Moving Beyond What I Left Behind

By

Carl W. Mohler

Copyright 2018

cmohlerjr@aol.com

Moving Beyond What I Left Behind

Moving Beyond What I Left Behind was the toughest decision that I have ever had to make as a bipolar person. The hardest task I had ever been faced with up to that point in my life was not just admitting to the world that I was imperfect, but admitting to the world that my imperfection was caused by being bipolar. It is a challenge just to admit to the world that you are bipolar, but when there is no solution to your problem the decision to share your imperfection can be catastrophic. However, with the aid of my medical treatment team, my life has become complete and I am moving beyond the horrors that turned my life upside down over twenty years ago. I have decided I will not be denied and that I will work extremely hard to regain everything I once lost...and then some. I am at that point in my life where I am realizing a new potential thanks to a new professional environment and a new medical treatment team. What I have found incredibly amazing is that I have a renewed faith in myself to recapture what I once lost.

I am not afraid to grow from my mistakes caused by being bipolar, yet I don't blame my setbacks on anyone else because it was not anyone else's fault in the world that I have this illness. My inadequacies can only rest with myself and if I fail to adjust it is only because I don't pay attention to my own learned behavior. If I don't learn from myself and I chose to grovel in my own ineptitude, then that would entirely by my fault. One personal weakness that I have chosen to improve on, as a result of the experience of writing my first book, was a lack of assertiveness towards and awareness of others...to be more aggressive and aware of others at the same time. Learning how to sell books again and interact with others called for the emergence of a new me and the generation of a new marketing force to be reckoned with. This was the beginning of a new destiny. I see this new destiny as a chance to help fulfill everybody's desires including my own. After being bipolar for twenty-five years, I have developed broad ambitions and goals I am not afraid to confront despite my illness. I am ready to Move Beyond What I Left Behind. This is my time not to be denied.

Bipolar disorder, also known as manic depression, is a common psychiatric disorder manifested as periods of extremely elevated mood and periods of depression. It is caused by an abnormality of the brain that leads to mood swings, swings in energy levels, and rapid swings in activity levels. In my own case, sometimes it would affect my cognitive level of ability to complete day to day tasks. Symptoms of the bipolar disorder may range in impact from mild to severe, and from extremes of ups and downs which can result in damaged relationships, poor jobs skills, or school performance, and in some cases, unfortunately, suicide. However, despite all the negative issues associated with being bipolar, many people with the illness can be treated and lead full and productive lives.

Mania is the word that describes the activated phase of the bipolar disorder. When it is less severe it is also called hypomania and this type of mania may manifest itself in a variety of forms. People on the high side of the bipolar disorder may feel that most of the time they are on top of things production wise, in being sociable, and self-confident. Many people have described that high of hypomania as being the ultimate high, better than any other time they have been feeling good in their life. However, their feelings are exaggerated and they can't understand why other people can't relate to this strong feeling in their life or to this part of their disorder.

Surprisingly, bipolar illness is not uncommon. Approximately three percent of the U.S. adult population has bipolar disorder. In the United States that is a mean average of about ten million people. This affects men and women equally. The risk of the bipolar illness usually occurs before the age of thirty-five. People between the age of fifteen and twenty-five are usually the most highly at risk. Unfortunately, children are becoming an extremely high-risk group as well. As those with bipolar disorder become more familiar with their illness, they recognize their own unique patterns of behavior. If individuals recognize the signs and seek effective and timely care they can often prevent relapses. Individuals who live with bipolar disorder also benefit tremendously from taking responsibility for their own recovery once the illness is adequately managed. They must monitor side effect changes in mood and changes in lifestyle. The healthcare provider should be willing to respond to changes in behavior with respect, changes in medication or any other fine tuning of treatment.

Recovery is an ongoing daily process. No one can manage an illness as well as the person that is living it every day. Sufferers should give themselves credit for having the courage to make the necessary changes in their life to survive the illness. Sufferers should acknowledge that this process is hard and that they must be determined to make any external changes in their lives. This allows for developing a balanced lifestyle that will help make changes in living and managing the bipolar disorder. It will help people take control of their illness and become an expert in managing it.

People with bipolar disorder usually experience emotional states that occur in distinct periods called "mood episodes" (mood liability). These episodes can go from an overly joyful (excessive laughter) or increased drive which in an excited stated can lead to a manic episode, sadness, or a state of depression. On many occasions, a mood swing is both manic and depressive. People with the bipolar disorder may also be explosive and irritable during a mood swing. Thus, my new voyage begins on my trail of tears to overcome the ups and downs of the bipolar disorder.

I have come to really think about how this whole issue spiraled out of control in my personal life, but it is very difficult to determine what caused my internal struggles throughout the years. How issues elevated to the point they did, I will never know and how the bipolar illness went on to become a major abnormality in my life at this point I will never know. However, it became such a paramount struggle for me that I was always at odds with it and it led to one major malfunction after another in my life. For the past twenty-five years this has been one negative experience after another that I have not been sure how to deal with, but hopefully that has become a thing of the past.

I really didn't recognize anything abnormal in my life as a child growing up. My brothers and I worked extremely hard as kids, but I had no regrets about the livelihood that I shared with them. I don't think it was the ideal situation, but I had no regrets about the way my parents raised me. I didn't think there was anything that caused any unusual stressors or anything unusual to indicate that I was abnormal. I guess there was only one major difference between myself and the neighborhood kids and that I wasn't really mechanically-inclined and I was unusually awkward on the athletic field. It made me feel somewhat socially awkward as well, but I had my academic pursuits to absorb me, so I really didn't care. I always had a constant desire to improve myself in the classroom because it was not a struggle for me as a teenager to do that, and many of my academic peers pointed me in that direction. My efforts paid off when I was inducted into the National Honor Society with great ease. At that point in my life, there was no indication from any source that I was bipolar, but this was all about to change after I left high school and went on to experience the stressors of college and the Army. I was about to find out the meaning of chaos! It was definitely a long-term learning process to get me up and beyond my illness, to where I knew I needed to be.

I learned that, even though I have a mental illness, there is nothing that should get in the way of what I want out of my life. I learned that I could conquer my mental illness and reach out to fulfill my professional goals. My present goal is to move forward and be the best possible person that I can be and to not compromise on issues that affect my individual integrity. I have learned that I can open myself up to the rest of the world and say "look, I am bipolar, but my life is fine despite that, and I am here to help those deal with the issue that they don't know how to deal with." Just because you have the label of being "bipolar" does not mean you should shirk from what you think you want to achieve out of life. A lesson I learned that I can pass on is that, even though I let the bipolar illness get the better of me in the military, I still have goals that I want to set for myself and I proved that I can make a better person of myself as a civilian.

One of my biggest mistakes in dealing with the bipolar illness was self-medicating to deal with the issue. I didn't realize how devastating that approach could be until it was too late. Self-medicating could make your worse traits become dominant and lead to a complete nightmare scenario. There were times when I wondered why I was so spontaneous and so obsessive compulsive. At times, I was a borderline jerk with the best of my friends. I just wanted to tell them what I was going through...my growing pains; but it was weekend after weekend with which I had to cope, whether as a civilian or a soldier. The medication seemed like it was the only way I could lose myself and somehow face the reality I was in or, more likely, to escape the reality I was in. As the nights wore on I just became more consumed with whatever would take the pain away. I would beg for it to stop, but the drive for the pure sweetness of foreign tasting liquors and other alcohol products would never go away.

At this point, I can't honestly say I was aware of abusing alcohol due to being bipolar, because there were a lot of drunk, obnoxious students on campus that didn't run around claiming they had a mental illness. I just knew my life was starting to deteriorate, and this deterioration was not going to go away as long as I had a desire to abuse myself through alcohol. I knew I was abusing alcohol, but I didn't know why I was abusing alcohol at that point. The thought of self-medication had not even crossed my mind. I just wish I had been enlightened enough to think of it in that fashion. I was starting to do some awkward and silly things, but I attributed that to being socially awkward and going through growing pains, trying out for different varsity sports or trying different academic programs that I didn't really have the academic aptitude to be pursuing. I never had any real success in anything until I decided to pursue what I really wanted to pursue.

As a freshman, and later as a sophomore, I made every attempt to be socially acceptable through being an athlete and joining a fraternity. I tried out for the soccer team both years. The coach could not have asked for a clumsier athlete! I got to touch the ball when we scrimmaged and in practice, but not after that. I guess this was partly due to the fact that I might not have applied myself hard enough from day to day due to the party I had attended somewhere on campus the previous night. Yes, I got caught up in the fraternity scene. I was not content to pledge one fraternity, but I had to pledge two in back to back years. Without question, something was definitely driving me to improve on my social life. It was a passion, a thirst, a desire...and it was fun. However, having such an intense social life put a financial strain on me. I was quick to realize that my availability of financial resources was headed south very quickly.

With the cost of tuition going up, I reacted quickly with a bold and brash plan in mind. I decided I was going to be daring and audacious and join the U.S. Navy. I wanted to brave the challenges of the nuclear community. To sail off over the seven seas would challenge any young man's commitment and resolve. I was very intelligent, but I was also very courageous and without reserve. Fortunately, somebody had better judgment than myself. The Dean of Students thought this professional development move may not be in my best interest, so one Saturday afternoon he and I had a long talk. Somehow, he persuaded me to stay in school and finish my degree and just overlook the armed forces for the short term (I didn't tell him about my intent to join the Army Reserve for the short term and use ROTC to pay for my degree). I don't think the Dean eventually minded that idea because ROTC was a closely managed program and the Dean knew it would keep me in school. The Dean of Students was a very intuitive man. I think he somehow knew there was something wrong with me from a medical standpoint. He just didn't know what to do about it in 1985, like everybody else. I needed to make more money to stay in school and the Reserves and ROTC was a conservative way to do it with minimal risk.

A part-time job would have reduced my stress level, and the College provided that. I really don't think that anybody realized that I had a mental illness, including me, at this point in time. I had to be a hero, and prove that I could deal with my issues, though I didn't fully understand them, and continue to move forward. It seemed I had my life together. I was working towards the degree I wanted, I had a part-time job I wanted where I was working as a supervisor, but I was still abusing alcohol and I didn't know why. I also wanted to make more money to stay in school, Finally, I had my chance to do that. My introduction to the Army Reserve and the ROTC program made all that possible and the Dean...well, he didn't say anything about my decision when it came to that. There was one kicker: the fact was that I had to go to basic training before I was allowed to contract with ROTC and make any of my financial and college dreams come true. I was in for a surprise.

It turned out that the Army was going to make life miserable for me as a private. I had to be a hero once again, and being the man that I was, I had to fulfill my contract even though I couldn't shoot to save my life (and there continued to be signs of my mental illness). The fact that I couldn't shoot to save my life was a rude awakening that I was about to experience in the world of ROTC and an even ruder awakening in the world of basic training. I went to basic training and I couldn't hit the broadside of a barn to save my life.

It was the first week in June at the MEPS station in Harrisburg, PA and I had just passed my physical and my ASVAB entrance examination. I was loaded on a commercial bus headed east for Ft. Dix, NJ. At that point I didn't hate my recruiter, but then again, I hadn't yet done a pushup or been called "Lurch." My positive feelings that I had for personnel that had sworn me into the Army would change within the next twenty-four hours. A joke surrounding the MEPs station was that you shouldn't waste time writing letters to your recruiter, but you should write letters to your mother instead. Your mother cared. Recruiters don't write back. I gave the NCO who told the joke the dirtiest look, but then realized that he was right. Welcome, to Ft. Dix, NJ; your home away from home for the next nine weeks. For me, since I was about to become the bolo king, it was going to be a long nine weeks. I thought that if Basic Training was anything like the processing station, it couldn't be too bad. Surprise, Surprise!

If I didn't know exactly what I was getting into, I was soon going to find out. The first week of basic training was spent in the reception station; which wasn't a bad way to go, I thought. Then it came! Day Six. Boys...LOVE IT OR LEAVE IT. Welcome to Basic Training: Third Platoon, Rock

Platoon, Best Platoon, Rock. Fifty-three privates strong were packed into the cattle truck, moving out for Bravo Company. That is where I should have quit, but I was standing tall and looking good and I should have been in Hollywood, so I stayed. Basic is where I met the meanest person in the world: the drill sergeant waiting for me to get off that cattle truck and to beat my face. His name was Pat Sirois and he was the leanest and meanest brown round that Chicago had ever produced. I flew off that truck so fast and before I knew it I was in the dirt with him beating my face like you wouldn't believe it. The man had my number and he was enjoying it all the way. He loved every minute of it.

I shot out of the barracks that morning like greased lightening into the company area. I had never seen such a mean and vicious person wearing a brown round. His name was Joe Simpson and if there were ever a man that could put the fear of God into a new soldier it was him. He looked me square in the eyes and said beat your face. After the abuse I had to take the previous day, I thought he was frickin' nuts. Then he looked at me real close and he said, Private, do you have a problem with communication or do I have to repeat myself... beat your face. I still looked at him like he was kind of half loco. I was really sizing up Drill Sgt. Simpson as if he was something really different from my previous experience. He looked at me one last time and he said I am going to make myself real clear this time. Drop and give me fifty. That I understood real quick even though I thought the order was a little extreme, but I didn't waste any time executing the order. I was very understanding by that point in time. Then my dear drill sergeant ordered me to sound off with my deep impression of Lurch with each completed push-up. Welcome to nine weeks of purgatory in which the whole company formation got to hear me do this three times a day. It was getting to the point where this wasn't fun anymore. This went on for about two weeks and then I got introduced to the next phase of the purgatory training that I was in and that was the arms room.

Week Three, Day One. The arms room opened up at 0645. Mohler with the number 965123. Plastic and metal hit my hands simultaneously for the first time in two weeks and the fear of God was put into me almost instantly. Why I was shaking so much was beyond me because this was only an M-16 A1 rifle. This weapon had been cleaned and cleared by the armorer before I had even touched it and nobody in the Army had said I was bipolar up to that point in time so, to me, this week should have been a piece of cake. What did I have to fear? The Army overlooks things when it comes to meeting a quota, so I can't say I had been taken advantage of. As the old saying goes, "as long as nobody gets hurt," ...maimed, or killed, but it didn't change the fact that I was afraid of my weapon. Let's face it. What really could go wrong at this stage? How could I not qualify? I thought that the numbers, theoretically speaking, were on my side.

It was Day Three of BRM week. By now, I had learned how to assemble and disassemble my weapon every which way imaginable. Now it was time for the battlefield zero and to head for the zeroing range. Assume the prone position, insert one three round magazine, place your selector switch on semi, and commence firing. Once you are done with your weapon, wait to be cleared off the range by a drill instructor. Once the range is cleared, move off down range at a range walk and prepare to zero your target and confirm a battlefield zero. I went to my target and I looked and I looked. Drill Sgt. Simpson came up behind me and scrutinized my target and said "Damn, son, what were you shooting at?" I knew this was going to be a long day. Twenty-one shots later, I still had not zeroed my weapon and Mr. Simpson was beginning to have a serious issue with me. I wished I was back in college. I was not in the Infantry yet, and I definitely was not shaping up to be in the Infantry! At zero dark hundred I was the last person to clear off the range and I was the only person that had not zeroed their weapon yet.

I just hung my head that night in the barracks. It had been a heck of a long day that I didn't want to think about any more. My roommate, Peter, could see that I was in a very sober state. If there was ever a night you wanted to get a letter from mom, this was it. She knew I had a hatred for weapons and she was aware of how focused this part of basic training was on weapons. I was only nineteen at the time and I wanted to study to get my doctorate in history. Killing people was not one of my goals. However, I was stuck, so I had to try and make the most out of my position in life. I smiled inwardly, and realized that there was always tomorrow, and the qualification challenges would resume. Oh, woe is me, I thought. I knew I had to succeed tomorrow. Bipolar or not, tomorrow I was not going to accept any excuses from myself. The command echoed in my ears once again. Lock and load one three round magazine, place your

weapon on semi, and prepare to zero.
Once again, I walked down the range
with Drill Sgt. Simpson to look at my
target. He wanted to see the results
more than I did. Sure enough, there
were three shots almost as tight as a
dime, dead center of the target. My
lessons from yesterday had been well
applied this morning. Simpson looked
at me like I was stupid and said get off
this man's range. I never range walked
so fast as what I did at that moment.
The question of the moment was,
would my streak of good luck hold for
the rest of the day, as I headed
towards the qualification range. Drama
and suspense were in the air as I
wondered if I could hope to avoid
another day of negative fate.

The sun broke over the horizon as I stared down the firing alley with targets ranging up to three hundred meters away. For some reason, I felt that this was my day. But I had a degree of self-doubt inside of me. I would have forty rounds at my disposal to hit twenty-three targets. The voice in the tower echoed out that morning. The officer in charge was all business that morning. I was shaking like a leaf, not knowing that it might be a bipolar tremor. The wartime commands were on the verge of being given. "Fires, assume your fighting position, lock and load one-ten round magazine, place your selector switch on semi, and prepare to defend your position." The word bolo echoed in my mind as I squeezed off my first round. I had defeated my cause before I even got started. Forty rounds later my inspiration definitely said bolo. I will refrain from repeating what Drill Sgt. Simpson said to me when he saw my scorecard other than beat your face. By this time in basic training I was becoming quite buffed. My confidence was shot by this point, but somewhere, somehow, I knew I could pull up that little extra to go the miles needed to be a success in this part of basic training.

I was rescheduled to go back to the range the following day. I kept to myself that morning and everybody in the platoon respected that, including Drill Sgt. Simpson. He knew I needed time to myself and I needed to relax and concentrate because this was probably the most important day of basic training for me. If I didn't qualify today it would be two days prior to graduation before I could try again. I was just kind of meandering that morning in the company area, when senior drill approached me and tried to give me a pep statement by saying I wasn't the best and I wasn't the worst he had ever seen. I really didn't want to bust the guy's ego at this point, but I just wanted to tell him I wanted to be left alone. But he was senior drill, so what can you do about it? How do you tell senior drill you don't want to be in another training cycle with him? Bipolar illness, which I didn't know I had, and I, were battling each other to get through basic training. I wanted to get back to what I commonly referred to as normalcy. I will admit that these "drills" were very intelligent infantry soldiers and incredibly intelligent men altogether, but outside of the world of the brown round, they really didn't have much going for them. I always had a mutual respect for my brown round. I always thought that there was a level of distinctiveness and integrity to the uniform, even though I had my moments in which I struggled.

Life in basic training wasn't complete without mom. I thought that I was growing into becoming a solid soldier without mom. But when I was slightly hypomanic at one point, I called my mother crying and very upset and my mother was not there to answer the phone. Later, my mother called my drill Sgt. and wanted to know why her big private was crying on the phone like a little baby. I didn't know why I was crying...I didn't have an answer, not knowing that I was bipolar. Maybe my only excuse for crying was that the range wasn't working in my favor which my mother and I had already discussed, but the manic release just came out of nowhere and nobody (including me) really understood why.

I thought that as a soldier I had it together. However, after I had "boloed" for the third time, I really began to have doubts. Then came the day of the brigade commander's inspection. He noticed that I didn't have a marksmanship badge on display. I had a tough time explaining why that was and I wasn't sure where to start. The brigade commander made it easy on me, he grabbed the barrel of my weapon and showed it to me. I just nodded and waited for him to leave, got out my cleaning kit and went to work on my barrel. My name was now mud in the eyes of my brigade commander. Life can really take a downturn in basic training when you least expect it, though I think Drill Sgt. Simpson was really cool about the whole incident. He knew the Col. had really gotten under my skin, but I had learned something from the experience. When he was satisfied that I had cleaned my weapon to standards, he ran me through the fundamentals of marksmanship again and again until he was satisfied that I would qualify the next day, hands down. For once I was not afraid of the unknown, because somebody else had instilled confidence in me at their own level despite my own thoughts of what it would take for me to be successful.

I was about to find out what it meant to over- compensate, and with only a day and a half until graduation. I did everything at a double time. I wanted to go back to college in the worse way. I was very crisp in every move I executed on the parade field that morning. I was standing tall and looking good and quickly fell into the position of parade rest when senior drill approached me. He looked me square in the eyes as if looks could kill. With ice in his veins, he very directly informed me that if I didn't qualify later that morning I would be recycled to the next training cycle...not going home, and not going back to college. My ass would be his for another nine weeks. Hostile language usually doesn't work on me, but coming from senior drill I was starting to shake in my boots a little bit. I couldn't imagine spending nine more weeks with a royal butthead like this.

It was getting very humid real fast as I loaded my goat smelling arse on the company truck later that morning. I was a solitary figure on the backend of the truck that morning and I wasn't saying anything to anyone, not even the driver, who was a drill. I think I even overcompensated on my prayers to God that morning. I always prided myself in being a thinker, but I wasn't sure how this was going to help me this morning. "Brains over brawn, but how?" I asked myself. Then it hit me when I least expected it. Reverse psychology! I had taken psychology in high school and in this case the scorer was the judge so you had to plead your case to the scorer and that is exactly what I intended to do. When we got to the firing range, I wasted no time and went directly to working on the scorer. For some reason, he was empathetic to my case. My drill was confused about what I was doing, and he was very angry that I was not focused on the targets down range. The officer in charge of the tower that day took charge and there was nothing that my drill could do about it from that moment on. From there forward it was just my scorer and me...and my scorer was on my side from that moment on. "Firer's assume the position, lock and load one ten round magazine, place your selector switch on semi, and prepare to defend your position." After forty rounds, I was cleared off the range with my scorecard and with my Drill Sgt. trailing a few feet behind. While he waited for my score card I did pushups in the sound. He got my scorecard and the score was 23 out of 40. He was stunned and angry at the same time. Mr. Sundeen's psychology class from New York Mills High School had bested the best leadership principles from the United States Army. On this day, my wit had won out.

My drill ordered me back on the truck and we hit the road as fast as that old GM could go. As soon as we hit the company area, the drill ordered me off the truck...and this time to clean my weapon right. Senior drill wasted no time coming over to see the score sheet and called me a lucky SOB. "I will see your tail tomorrow." I was going to be standing tall and looking good on the parade field out there one last time. I had beat the Army system with my own form of the buddy system, and what a feeling that was. I would get to march in a graduation ceremony that was probably going to go equally as well as my testing. Dressed in class B's, the Drill Sergeants led the platoon past the reviewing stand. I I had never felt more proud in my professional career than what I did at that point in my life. I felt like I had really accomplished something worthwhile. I had risen to the challenge of "be all you can be" despite the unknown challenges of a disability, and I felt like a million bucks again. As a result, I was plagued by a profound confusion for once in my life. I had initially thought I wanted to go back to college, but I wasn't sure at this moment if it was for me. The Army had allowed me to escape from the insanity of being in college, so maybe this was the best option for me. The timing was not good for decision-making. Perhaps if this was an issue I had addressed two weeks prior to graduation I might have made up my mind a lot quicker.

While I was momentarily confused, a quick hug from my parents caused me to snap to. I was always my mother's little boy, but I have a lot of respect for my father as well. However, a quick handshake from a strong-willed Drill Sgt. restored my military bearing very quickly. He gave me a compliment for a job well done which left me grinning from ear to ear. This probably was the event that made me feel like a real man for the first time in my life. Despite this renewed energy and vigor, I was about to go through a period of delayed adjustment when I reported back to college for soccer camp. I wondered if I even adjusted at all, thanks to the abusive drinking that I quickly picked up upon returning to college. I still didn't know that I was bipolar at this time, I just felt troubled and I was abusing alcohol to cover up everything. I used it as a crutch or an excuse to cover up negative or inappropriate behavior. I became torn in college that year. I worked extra hard on the field, but I kept on reminding myself that I now had a scholarship that I had to keep myself in contention for, a big scholarship. I made my final career choice for degrees this year and surprisingly enough ROTC even went along with it. Jumping from degree to degree left me very unsettled and I thought I was spending too much time going from professor to professor seeking one-on-one mentoring...a positive move if you have the aptitude to stay in the degree, but I had just reached the point where I was acting out of frustration and not satisfaction. The bottom line was that I was satisfied with my new career choice and so was ROTC (shocker) and I was going to ride this choice out for the next two and a half years through graduation and commissioning as an Adjutant General Officer. It worked for me at this point in my life, so it seemed that is all that mattered. The most important thing was that it left my mind content, even though I was still using alcohol to self-medicate. My new career choice really improved me all the way around.

ROTC allowed me to fulfill my degree and get my commission. I gained a new purpose in life because of my commission, even though I thought I felt I was inadequate on many fronts. I was left with a positive attitude in so many different directions, despite potential setbacks associated with my undiagnosed bipolar illness. I had made mistakes in the ROTC program, but there had been a lot of positive moments for me, so I took great pride in my accomplishments. Even though I could not qualify to save my life, I took great pride in the fact that the US

Army wanted me on active duty in my branch of choice for my leadership. It took a tough positive attitude to offset my weaknesses and to get assessed on active duty while being bipolar. I didn't know I was bipolar at the time they assessed me on to active duty and I think if I would have known I would have turned down the assignment unless I was getting some type of treatment. I was aggressive and forward, but not reckless. Even though I prided myself in being a leader, I didn't pride myself in being a fool at the same time. I wanted active duty, but not at the price I later paid when I was on active duty. I would have gladly swallowed my pride for the sake of my health if that would have been a clear decision to make. Looking back, despite the poor decision to go on active duty, I had a lot of fun with ROTC. It gave me a lot of polish as a citizen soldier and gave me the drive and desire to find a separate identity for myself and to aggressively pursue something different; something that very few other people did with their lives. I was proud to be a lieutenant at this point in my life.

All great fairy tales begin with the words "once upon a time." This one is no exception from beginning to end. But to put a timeline in place to this odyssey is very difficult. It is also very difficult to make readers understand the growing pains I went through along the way. I found that growing up as a bipolar person can be quite degrading as well. Over the past twenty-two years the disease has pushed my personality and stamina to demonic and unreasonable heights without any major notice from people around me, or that was my perception, anyway. I always wondered if my perceptions about myself had any value or were true to any degree.

Out of all the concentrations available in the History Department, I enjoyed Military History the most because of my experience in the Army Reserves and my exposure to the campus ROTC program. My introduction to the Army Reserves and the Army ROTC program opened up a whole new career field for me. I think, for the first time in my live, I felt anger about not recognizing this sooner. ROTC was like an introduction to corporate America at a micro level that would pay dividends years later when I went on active duty as a commissioned officer. I even knew that my first paycheck as a lieutenant was going to be substantially more than what I had earned in the Reserves or in ROTC (a motivating factor in itself). Even though I was only a private at the time (at the low end of the pay scale), I knew all my hard work would eventually be rewarding. It wasn't all about hard work though. I did have a good time at jockeying tanks around in the motor pool in the dead of winter, sleeping while standing up in the gunner's hatch manning the coax in the dead of night. The weekend drill always gave me a reason to drink when I got back to campus, in order to vent my aggressive behavior.

My overly aggressive behavior was not really apparent to me at this point in time. I do not know what possessed me to want to be involved in barbaric acts such as flesh-piling my friends, but I openly participated if it appeared there was no wrong in the matter. But apparently there was, Years later I would regret the friendships that were lost due to such childish acts.

Along with ROTC entering my life, I had to cope with coming home from basic training. The biggest challenge I had was with my aggressive behavior. The complaints began as soon as I got back to campus. It was not only assertive behavior, but I had gone so far as to furnish my dorm room with everybody else's furniture. It was amazing how crooked my room loft had become while I was trying to put it up and drink a six-pack at the same time. I couldn't hit a nail straight if you paid me to. But I wanted to be a hero one last time, so I tried out for the soccer team under a new coach. I made the squad, but practicing day in and day out with a hangover did not help my situation any. I had to be everything to everybody, expecting only a beer or two in return to satisfy my deepest desires. I knew things were out of control, especially when the Dean of Students called me into his office just to slow me down and advise me that things would be fine. At that point, he did not know I had developed a strong appreciation for Coors Light and that my social life probably would have fallen apart without it.

Things eventually went as the Dean had said they would, except for the drinking issue. My major was agreeable with my academic talents; I liked it; and I had a method of paying for college, with a future profession waiting for me after graduation. I was a supervisor in conference/food services, and I belonged to a fraternity without anybody questioning my drinking habits or the fact that I might have an illness, except for me. Although this never happened, I wish somebody had been able to tell me I was bipolar. I can't put an exact finger on it, but this time frame was probably about when the illness took root. I had become truly aggressive in my work practices and somewhat defiant. I tried too hard to be socially defiant throughout my growing years and in my work life. Several people started to become concerned, but not me. I was going down the path of self-destruction, but I just didn't realize it.

There were so many different events that transpired during my last four semesters of college that were like escalating factors that increased the likelihood that my condition might take a turn for the worse. What scared me the most, to this day, was that I didn't know I was bipolar, until seven years after my college experience. There were so many different points at which the bipolar illness could have taken a turn for the worse that I can only consider myself to be extremely fortunate things didn't get worse. I am fortunate the binge drinking did not blow up on me psychologically. It is easy to sit here and apologize to the people who may have been hurt by me throughout the years and may have mixed emotions about me at this point, but I can't gauge the pain and misunderstanding I may have caused friends and families while I was going through my growing pains with the bipolar disorder.

My last two years of college focused around the Reserve Officers Training Corp, classes, supervising food service employees, and binge drinking. I wanted to let go of the drinking so badly, but I knew if I did I would be facing almost immediate disaster, from what extreme I didn't know, but at a minimum it would probably mean losing my scholarship and joining Alcoholics Anonymous. Only God would know what other catastrophes would emerge at that point as well.

A side aspect of the bipolar disorder is that the patient may exhibit obsessive-compulsive behaviors. I got involved with weightlifting and deadlifting to stay focused--perhaps *overly* focused--at this time in my life.

My drive and desire kept me moving forward until I was deadlifting 500 pounds and bench pressing 295 pounds. I can only guess how much I was squatting then as well. I was continually obsessed to try to push myself harder and harder every day. I worked out with the football team twice a day, plus I was creative enough to invent exercises on my own. I exercised with my friend Igor, who pushed me to my max every day. From day to day, I became more and more exuberant as my abilities to compete at higher levels steadily improved. Despite the alcohol diet which consumed me on a daily basis, I would not stop anything I was doing. I didn't know if I was making any friends during this period. I just knew I had a need; that need was to succeed.

In training with the Reserve Officers Training Corps, I also found more than one reason to push myself beyond acceptable limits. I spent three days a week doing road work; another two days were spent biking. All of this was done on top of all the time I spent in the gym. It was pure insanity at its best. I pushed myself not only to where I was tearing my body apart, but I was also delaying the healing process of an old injury I had suffered in Airborne school. I had to have arthroscopic surgery on my knee just to give me a fighting chance to stay in ROTC. After the surgery, it was a question mark as to whether I would be allowed to earn my commission. I worked endless hours with the athletic trainer at college to get back on the right track. Hot/warm treatments twice a day, in addition to a less rigorous workout until I got permission from the trainer to resume the insane abuse I was putting on my body. Along with one of my fellow classmates, I was on the verge of making history at school in another year; I didn't want to shortchange myself out of all my hard work. A lot of tax dollars had been poured into my degree and into my professional development to become a commissioned officer. Honestly, to be truthful, some of it had gone into my habits of self-medicating myself. As much as I tried to fight it at that point, the bipolar illness was slowly, ever so slowly starting to erode away at my mental capabilities and beginning to surface.

However, right then, my symptoms were very subtle. My energies were challenged and my obsessive-compulsive behavior, which caused me to do a lot of relatively reckless things, had been bridled. Unfortunately, I displayed a lot of channeled aggressive behavior towards my friends in the form of overly physical contact and a desire to dominate. I had overcome the physical setback with my knee, and I was ready for one final major hurdle as a prelude to being commissioned. I prepared for Reserve Officers Training Corps Advanced Camp at Fort Bragg, North Carolina, home of the 82nd Airborne. However, I couldn't be just your contemporary airborne cadet. I had to be a hero and drive down to North Carolina instead of flying down. Thinking ahead of myself, I thought I would have the use of my vehicle on the weekend, but to my chagrin my truck was locked up behind concertino wire for the duration of camp. The weekend prior to graduation I was allowed to take my truck out and make a quick snack run to Burger King, then have about sixty minutes worth of liberty off the base. The night prior to having access to our vehicles, our platoon of cadets had a party at the local military canteen to celebrate our graduation. Once again, like a fool, I allowed my body to become saturated with alcohol, which very quickly dehydrated me. I staggered back to the barracks when, as luck would have it, I stumbled upon the platoon tactical officer, Capt. Hutchinson, who was just about the last person I wanted to be running into at that point. His job was to evaluate cadets to see if they were fit for active duty. At that juncture, even though I knew I was a very prolific writer and speaker, I also knew I wasn't the best. He liked the fact that I was very devoted to my duties, and clear and concise in my writing skills, but he didn't like seeing me abuse alcohol on the eve of graduation. As I looked into his eyes, I felt that whatever chance I had of getting a recommendation for active duty had been defeated by my own professional negligence.

As the six weeks had progressed through Advanced Camp, although Capt. Hutchinson and I had developed a mutual admiration for each other's wit and savvy, my skills as a soldier left something to be desired. Basic training could only teach a person so much about being a leader. There was not enough time for me to improve to the acceptable levels I desired, much less what Capt. Hutchinson wanted. My wit and intelligence had carried the day on many occasions, and in all likelihood had kept me out of a combat arms branch which would have gotten me or someone under my command killed.

I was not fully aware something was wrong with me as of then; I just knew I had a conscience--if there was anything wrong with me and I could go to any extreme to identify myself as being bipolar, I would have, but I was only a young man with a degree in History and soon to become a 2nd Lieutenant. If only I had known then what I know now, my life would have been a lot different.

The issue of marksmanship came up again. By this time I was wondering if anybody other than me was following trends throughout my history on the range. At that point we were given a few rounds to practice with. I took my first shot. My scorer said, "Bolo." Then I threw a rock at the target, and the scorer said, "Hit." It was going to be one of those days. Forty rounds later I had hit the targets 28 times. I wasn't completely sure, but I think Capt. Hutchinson was starting to notice a pattern. Yet there was nothing concrete about my different types of behaviors as of right then. One thing that *did* begin to stand out, however, was the fact I was experiencing mental exhaustion. My brain at some point seemed to be crying out for relaxation, which in wartime is a luxury you will not receive. My fellow classmates (platoon members) were trying to be as nice as possible concerning the issue, but I just couldn't hang in there at times. To be candid, I was ashamed of myself. For the first time since I had donned the uniform, I felt like I was openly abandoning my duty. We had adopted a tool from basic training called the Z-Monster. Every time I was lax, I was punished with him by others in the platoon. After weeks of somebody slapping me upside the head, I was ready to fight for something that was beyond my control. I was to damn my soul, but there was nothing I could do about it.

Fort Bragg was a true adventure. That was where I learned to become a true leader and to deal with the issues surrounding the bipolar illness for the next few years. I didn't know that one day the demon in me would be unleashed somewhere or somehow. I knew something was wrong, but I didn't know what. I just knew the current mission was to evaluate me for active duty, which is what I got when I received my first "branch of choice" in the Army. It was time to be a hero. The true test of me being able to control the mental exhaustion associated with the bipolar illness was with the company's field training exercise. Even though I had performed as a leader and I had shown potential, I had failed at almost every aspect of my soldiering skills, due to my bipolar illness. For once, Capt. Hutchinson showed disdain rather than concern. Despite my vigor and energy, I knew I was about to be lectured on my lack in professional judgment. Oddly enough, the lecture did not come on the night when I most expected it, but on the last night of Advanced Camp after I had had a chance to rest and clear my head.

I shake my head as I type this. After all these years, the memories still have not faded. I recall the good captain looking at me and shaking his head with so much doubt in his expression that I could clearly sense it. With a sigh, he just asked me point blank what I had expected out of Advanced Camp. I was firm in my reply. I would never quit being a hero, bipolar or not. "Sir," I said, "with all due respect and honesty, I would like active duty, but down deep I realize, after personally reviewing my own performance, I know you can't make that recommendation. If you can't make that recommendation, I would at least like to be given my branch of choice."

I had put the gentleman in a rather difficult position. Instinctively, I knew I was not going to get any of my choices. Why did I have to be so naïve at that point? Then for a reason that I didn't instinctively understand, he dimmed the lights in the tactical office because I was squinting excessively. He didn't say a word right then. He just politely dismissed me with my evaluation, which I wasn't so sure I wanted to read. However, it didn't turn out to be as negative as what I thought it was going to be. It said that he was impressed with my ability to write and communicate, but beyond that, he thought the only thing I would offer to active duty was leadership. Well, at least I was doing something right, I thought to myself.

My journey home from Ft. Bragg was completely uneventful, except for a downpour of rain which nearly put my truck in a ditch. I was quite reckless in my drive home. Sometimes I came close to revving my engine up to 85 miles per hour. I didn't realize that I hadn't checked the oil on my vehicle when I left Ft. Bragg, which could have been disastrous on the drive home. I was always the absent-minded person when it came to doing that. It would go on to cost me two blown engines on that truck at a later POINT in time due to my negligence, but at least Advanced Camp was over. It had been one learning experience I would never forget.

My senior year in college brought all kinds of chaos into my life--from what I now perceive to have been caused by the bipolar illness. I did such insane things that year, all the way from off-road trucking to becoming an assistant pledge master for my fraternity, a position I kind of abused. Either that or

I was sort of in an uncontrolled manic state at the time, which might have explained my uneven temperament.

My ability to pay attention to detail had really begun to plummet. While we had a positive break in the weather that spring, the Blue Mountain Battalion (from Dickinson College) had scheduled a field training exercise. The cadets had just completed a land navigation course. The day had gone extremely well for me until I set my compass down on a stump and walked away from it. Within seconds the tactical officer noticed I didn't have my compass and jumped on my case almost instantly. Another cadet and I were instructed to go searching for the compass. Mr. Dan Pagano, I apologize for dragging you two miles down that icy trail to compensate for my shortcomings. I was even more embarrassed when a freshman came jogging down the trail and told me the compass had been found. I maintained my silence until I got back to the dormitory that night. I had made a cardinal mistake and didn't know what had come over me that day.

The military was not the only place where I suffered due to a lack of diligence. I was shocked by the mental mistakes I was making in school as well. The worst part was that these chronic mistakes were beginning to cost me dearly. To compound matters at this point, I continued to drink. I felt like I was a clinical experiment with no guidance. I couldn't blame anybody but myself. Somehow, every morning I was hoping to get newfound relief, but it never came.

Despite the fact that it seemed as if none of my peers reached out to help me, I had a strong focus on my classes and my future career. My history classes kept me motivated, even though I marched forward without having recognized I was bipolar. My personal enjoyment of my degree kept me motivated with the willpower to succeed in my academics.

The biggest day of my life, and probably the highlight of my academic career, came in the spring of 1989 when I graduated and took my Oath of Office. History had been made at the school for the first time since the college had invited the Reserve Officers Training Corps to play an active role in the development of student leadership. As far as the bipolar illness was concerned, I thought this was the beginning of the end. However, my career as a professional soldier was about to spin out of control. The next twenty-two years of my life were about to create new challenges which I couldn't foresee. I can't fully relay this story to you, due to the pain and challenges I had to endure. But the purpose in writing this document has been to help individuals who have had to deal with bipolar illness, whether they are enduring it alone or with the help of the support groups that exist for them. I want others to see how much work it takes to help individuals with the bipolar illness to lead successful lives.

My next stop before going to Germany was the Adjutant Officer's Basic Course at Fort Harrison, Indiana. This was what I trained for; this was the reason ROTC invested in me with a three-year scholarship to go to college; this was where my leadership was about to pay off. I had taken the summer off to help my father with his business and I had come away a rejuvenated soul. A summer away from the rat race allowed me to finally spend time learning to be content with my soul and finding peace and tranquility in everything I did. My father paid me well that summer and even though it was a blue-collar labor job, I enjoyed it immensely. Being on top of the corporate world really meant nothing to me at age twenty-two because I knew I was going to be on top in the

Army in a few short months when I began my tour of duty. I should have been content at that point in my life because my life was controlled. If I'd remained in the States as a working man I probably would have found out about the bipolar issues at a more graduated pace than what I did when I went to Europe. The misery it would have saved me! But I was twenty-two and very excitable and I wanted to experience the world. I had orders in hand and I was ready to excel to the best of my ability once again. My report date was October 14th, 1989 to the schoolhouse at Ft. Harrison. This was my chance to prove that I was worth the time that the military had invested so heavily in me. I wouldn't be denied (As I write this, I am sitting here smirking, because I am forty-six now and I still think back to my glory years at Ft. Harrison, thinking I need to live up to those same expectations. Something tells me I can still do it. Regardless of the fact that I am not supervising any military personnel anymore and I do not have enough hours in the day to drive myself to that level of expectation, I keep on thinking it should be a piece of cake). Anyway, when I got to Ft. Harrison, I was as giddy as a new school boy. I didn't notice the effects of my undiagnosed bipolar illness in the short term, as my body kind of reminded me that this was the appropriate way to act.

The first week at Ft. Harrison went fine except for the fact I started to drink again. Once stress built up and it aggravated my condition, I didn't hesitate to go to the officer's club and release my aggravation. I damn the day I ever started drinking again, even though it felt like it was subduing my condition. I was just fooling myself to believe that. I was just laying the groundwork for a lot of things to go wrong in the future because I couldn't refrain from drinking. I was always a wishful thinker at any given moment. But I think today of all the positive things that would have went right in my life if I had not started drinking at all. I know I can't blame this whole situation on the Army because the Army was not the one holding the bottle to my lips and drinking. Even though it is easy to go back and point fingers and blame the Army for something as trivial as this, both parties in this case settled the score with each other some time ago and we moved on. I enjoyed some years of professional success and the Army went on to win several more wars without me. I will admit that at the age of twenty-four I didn't even know what the word psychoanalysis was, but I had to have had some psychological insight about how some things worked in the world. I hope I had some degree of critical thinking by that point. (I am smiling again at this point, because I have a chance to rebuild what I lost seven years ago and to really feel good about life again).

Once again, I set myself up to be the bolo King. The king of all marksman that could not hit the broad side of a paper barn, even if you paid him to. This quickly became a class project and not just an individual effort to qualify. New glasses, binoculars, throwing stones. Finally, out of desperation, the cadre of members of my OBC class took me to a very isolated range. I was given 480 rounds of 5.56 mm ammunition. The command was given, lock and load one – ten round magazine, place your selector switch on semi, and prepare to defend your position. This was all too familiar. I couldn't see to save my life so with almost five hundred rounds of ammunition I was just going to blow away my target board. Four hundred and eighty rounds later I had hit the target twenty-six times which was the minimum amount required to qualify in the United States Army. I still remember this whole affair like it was yesterday even though I don't recall a single one of the tactical officers that were with me at that point in time. There were approximately three years left in my Army contract after that and that was the last time I qualified. Not only did the whole Army not realize I was bipolar, nobody realized I was suffering from glaucoma either. Between those two illnesses, I couldn't ever get it together when it mattered the most. However, I had something the Army wanted. It was hard to imagine that the Army was hard up for real leadership and that was something that I had plenty of. Then the day came: our orders were in and yours truly was not going to Germany to become a part of a war making PSC. I got rerouted to go to the nation of Belgium as the Community Adjutant for the NATO/Shape Support Group. It was to be its own mini hell within my life. They wanted me for my leadership, and if it wasn't for my illnesses that is exactly what they would have received.

Mons, Belgium. Stage Right

I had been in the transient facility for over a week and the stress and the boredom of adjusting to the new job along with not having anything to do was driving me stir crazy. I needed something to do, but the question was: Where? It was almost night-fall so I headed out on the economy not knowing what to expect. It was kind of a foolish thing to do, and I did it with hesitation. About three blocks up from the hotel, I ran into a little bar called the Red Lion. I had to go in and to my chagrin the bar was full of bikers and railroad workers and I was piped. I didn't know if I should stay, but in seconds everybody offered me a beer. That answered that question real easy like. I thought "Wow, this is better than America." I will defend this country anytime. About that time, I was six foot-four and 235 pounds with fifteen-inch pythons. I was ready for action. Everybody that was drunk and wanted to arm wrestle took real quick notice of me and within seconds a big burly guy, kind of out of shape though, challenged me. Within seconds I had defeated him real easy like and I had another round of beers thrust my way. I was beginning to feel this was my kind of place, even though I was in the military hierarchy. I mean: who would know? It took me about three hours of arm wrestling to become completely drunk and within three weeks I was best friends with everybody in the Red Lion. I thought this was the best three weeks that I spent anywhere in all of Belgium.

Chievres Airbase, stage left.

I didn't understand. I thought I was a shoe-in for my first promotion in the Army. All lieutenants got promoted at least once, except for me. I didn't know I was bipolar and nobody told me before I went on active duty. I thought young company grade officers were supposed to drink and be merry, but in my case, I was drinking to self-medicate. Unfortunately, I was drinking abusively and quite excessively. I just didn't understand why I had to be like this. I didn't want to hurt anybody, I just wanted to have a good time with my friends after getting off duty every night, and to drown my sorrows after a stressful day in the office. Another thing I didn't understand was why I had to be so impulsive and reckless. That was a question that could not answer, no matter how hard I tried. I even thought the game of pool was a challenge that had to be mastered. There was nothing smooth about me at this point in my life. I was just bold and reckless. I had no regard for anybody else, but everyone else cared about me and I was too ignorant to realize that. I never prided myself for being vain, but I would guess that this is one time that I really was vain, and my friends realized it. I was not only hurting myself, but I was hurting them when I completely ignored them when they were trying to tell me about how shallow I was being. I enjoyed their company, but I still don't think that they or I realized that I had a mental illness.

Then it hit. It had been a rather stressful day in the office and my performance had been rather lackluster and subpar all day. Despite everything, I had tried to be diligent about my duties, but to little avail. My commander had unintentionally embarrassed me in the office over a very sensitive personnel action that I was dealing with in a very conservative manner. All I had to do was ensure that it was in line with Army regulation for administrative accuracy, but I decided to take upon myself and review the Commander's part as well. He was the special court martial convening authority for five nations and I was going to empower myself with that authority as well. I got an A for initiative but an F for judgment. To make a long story short, the Colonel was more than upset, and then he informed me that I was expected to attend a dress blues community dinner that night because I was the community adjutant. Down deep I knew this was not the thing for me to do for the evening. I just knew something was wrong and I couldn't put my finger on it to save my life. I hoped that somebody had the right answer for me before the evening was out.

Then it had to happen. This is one memory that I hate to relive, but for the sake of clarifying how devastating the bipolar illness is, I feel compelled to share it. I had just purchased a brand-new Plymouth sports coupe from the local retail dealership and I had not had it for more than a month. I was experiencing what I now know were some manic ups and downs and I had decided that self-medication was the best thing for me at that point in time to help me tolerate the situation. I was a time bomb on a delayed fuse. When I descended upon the dining room that evening, the first place I went was the bar. My head was spinning and I was confused. I thought the only thing I could do to clear my thoughts was to indulge in a clear and delicious Belgian beer that was not less than nine percent alcohol. I needed to lose myself and my mistake was that I decided to lose myself real fast. My brain was on fire. I was cycling information so quickly, combined with the intensity of the alcohol, that I just wanted to flee from the party instead of becoming a part of it.

Two other company grade officers saw that I was going to probably need help for the rest of evening. They confronted me and tried to get me to surrender my keys. By then, my speech was slurred and I was flushed with anger. I could not understand why I was doing this to myself. My judgment was off-base and I had no consideration for my friends or my cohorts in uniform. To this day, I am ashamed of my behavior that evening.

I refused to surrender my keys and I refused to listen to anybody else's reasoning. I only wish I could have that ten minutes of drunken infamy back again. My imagination started running wild and kicking into high gear. I imagined that I had to go to Brussels on a top-secret mission to deliver some encoded paperwork. My thoughts were definitely shooting off on a tangent at this point. To make matters worse, I had not yet surrendered my keys and I had not listened to anybody else's advice. I didn't understand why I had to be a hero that night.

Being the unfocused hero that I was, I jumped into my car to pursue a secret mission that only I could justify. Ole Miss to creativity I was. This is a tough one to share, but I'm going to, because everyone that suffers from emotional distress needs to be aware of how frazzled their behavior can be without being on the proper medication. At this point in time, the only medication I was on was alcohol. I sped on to the auto route going to Brussels and I didn't hesitate to take my little sports coupe up to 85 mph. To make matters worse, it was raining quite heavily. So everything that could go wrong was probably on the verge of going wrong. Let your imagination run with this...it did go wrong. My car ruptured a tire and within in seconds I had driven my car off the highway into a tree that was substantially bigger than my car. The only thought racing through my mind at that point was that I was going to die; nothing else. I had totally lost control of my car, but probably saved my life by letting go of my steering column and covering up my head and face as I crashed into the tree. The tree cracked my chassis straight down the middle of the car. The only thought I had then was that I had died and then the explosion of the airbag bought me back to reality. I felt an incredible pain shoot up the right hemisphere of my head that was going to haunt me for the next twenty years. Yes, I was going to pay the price for this mistake for the next twenty years of my life. I crawled out of the wreck of the car, and for some silly reason I thought I had to bring my briefcase with me.

I just sat there totally stunned; my head between my knees. I had totally messed up. My career was over. I had committed a DUI while in uniform in a foreign country. I was not fit to lead, much less take care of myself. I was just out of it. If I had any wit left within me I didn't know where it was. I just wondered how I could have been so ignorant. I just sat there and shook my head. I was finished, and I knew I was finished. But for some idiotic reason I felt it was necessary for me to go out as a fighting champion. Within seconds, I heard sirens over the horizon and my thought was I was not going to let them see me sweat. I was still the Adjutant of the NATO/Shape Support Group until Col. John T. Eanes said otherwise, and that had not happened yet.

I don't know how I passed the breathalyzer test. Despite my bravado,

I thought at that point that I could do nothing right. But Lady Luck must have been looking upon me favorably at that point, because I had not been charged with anything. Either the gendarmerie were impressed with my uniform or I lied to avoid the test. At this point it really doesn't matter, I just felt like I could do nothing right. I just know I had not been charged but I was too drunk to realize it. I am shaking my head as I type this. I've never forgiven myself for the atrocity that I committed that night. All of this just because I didn't know how to manage being bipolar or act responsibly in handling this mental health issue. I didn't know what the word psychiatrist was, and I am sitting here damning myself for not paying closer attention in my psychology class instead of being hung over every night that semester. I might have been able to psycho-analyze myself before the accident ever occurred, but I didn't. I was fortunate enough to have survived something that many others do not, bipolar or not.

The hero of the evening was Lieutenant Kim Johnson. I don't think she realized the full impact of what she did for me that night. I was stunned, in shock, not really aware of anything. I knew I wanted to flee from the scene of the wreck, but I had no fight left in me and Kim was the only person I knew in the area. I would not listen to anyone in the emergency room of the hospital. The ER doctor tried to rationalize with me, but I was still hung over and I was well beyond the point of listening. I was obsessed with getting out of the hospital because the only person that spoke English was the ER doctor himself. My head was spinning, and I was not aware of the severity of what the doctor was telling me. Concussions were nothing to mess around with, but I thought I was the heroic adjutant and I could deal with anything. I thought I was impervious because I had a security blanket. I was still in uniform and I had Kim's phone number in my briefcase and I was hoping she would take it upon herself to come and bail me out at first opportunity. I was asking a tremendous amount of my friend and I never did properly thank her for her heroics that evening because I had to be so macho the entire evening. I would give the world to have my dear friend Kim back in my life again.

I just couldn't understand how I could have been so reckless. I was in my dress blues, yet I was drinking and driving. I didn't even know what a breathalyzer was until that night. I really don't understand how I passed the test at all.

My confusion did not stop there. Instead, my irrational behavior continued on throughout the night. I finally called Kim around 2 AM to tell her what had happened. The ER staff wanted to keep me at the hospital for the rest of the evening for observation, but I had to be stubborn about it. The night had been nothing but a comedy of errors thus far, so I might as well keep on rolling while I was ahead of the ballgame, or so I thought. I was full of command decisions. As soon as Lieutenant Johnson showed up, I elected to leave the ER. The rage inside of me kept on building; I couldn't believe I had been so foolish.

I was a fool and I knew it. My choice of words was undesirable to say the least. I am hanging my head right now as I think about it. I somehow knew I was combatting a personal demon inside of me, but I could not convince anyone this was the case. I think it hurt more that I just couldn't bring myself to face the truth about the personal demon inside of me. When my friend Kim showed up and took me back to her place, she tried to help me calm my nerves. It was a hopeless task. It took hours before my temper began to subside.

Finally, she offered me a cup of tea, which calmed my nerves and slowly began to take effect. I was still very keyed up. I thought I had to be a superman one last time by returning to duty the next morning. I couldn't accept the fact I had screwed up so much. This was going to royally haunt my remaining time in uniform and cost me a promotion I had worked very hard to obtain. I can't fault the military for denying me my promotion. Honestly, I don't know who to blame for the mental anguish I had to endure right then. I was taking this adjutant thing way too seriously and I was only defeating myself.

Somehow, I convinced Lieutenant Johnson to take me back to the headquarters building the following morning. We both had to be there for duty. She tried to persuade me not to go, but I snapped at her and she backed away. She had been up the whole night trying to doctor me. If there was a true hero in this story, it was Kim. At that time, I don't know if she still considered me as her friend, because I wouldn't listen to her. If I had not been so bull-headed, my military career might have taken a turn for the better with Kim's help. She could have helped me become a first-rate officer with a flag grade career, even though I was bipolar.

While Kim shuttled me back to the Headquarters' building, I began to realize how mortal I was. I had to confront the commander about what had happened the previous evening. You'd think if I had had any common sense I would have waited a day to rest up a little bit. No, not me.

Kim was still thinking of me right up to the end. She wanted to go into his office with me, but I would have none of it. This was not her ass-chewing to take; it was mine. My career was ruined, but I was going to go down with my head held high, no matter how much pain I was in. The concussion pounded through my head that morning. I barely had the ability to maintain my focus on the commander. If I had ever addressed Col. Eanes appropriately, it was that morning, even though I could barely focus on pronouncing my words correctly. He looked at me directly. His eyes burned into my soul as he sternly and directly said, "Lieutenant, you messed up royally."

Generally speaking, untreated bipolars don't listen to anything their peers say and I was no exception. I was such a masochist at that point in my life. I was overly competitive, no matter what the obstacle. I had no fear where I should have turned the other cheek and walked away. I tried to tell myself that I was doing the righteous thing the following morning by being a true man and having walked into my bosses office and told him about the blunders of the evening. He probably thought I was the biggest fool and nobody had exercised so much poor judgment all at one time. If that is what he was thinking, he was right. I just openly told him what happened without any regard to my personal or professional well-being. I could have, legally, been stripped of my rank on the spot, but I was acting with a clear conscience. On that day I became a soldier, a bipolar soldier, but still a soldier. That is one lesson in life I never cared to repeat.

I didn't know what to say. I was getting more depressed by the moment. Perhaps this was the start of the mood swing I didn't know about, along with everything else. Undoubtedly, the concussion had triggered manic-depressive behavior. No matter how hard I tried to fight the pain I was in, it was an uphill battle which I had no chance of winning. My day in purgatory was about to begin, and my eternal hell was about to take another step forward that afternoon.

The group had a five-mile run scheduled for that afternoon. I was about to discover what post-concussion pain was all about. My eyes were watering and my voice was choking as I sounded off with the adjutant's call. I couldn't concentrate on anything as I attempted to do the adjutant's walk. The pounding in my head intensified more and more with each passing second as the words ricocheted in the right hemisphere of my brain. Somehow, I choked out my commands while my dear friend Kim looked on. She was almost in tears. Out of all the friends I have made in and out of the military, Kim had earned a place in my heart that is second to none. To this day I will never forget what Kim did for me that night. Because of using a little common sense, she somehow salvaged my military career for a few more years before I had to make a hard decision and leave the service myself. Kim helped me grow up into becoming a man sooner than expected. Through her mentoring I learned to take a little more serious responsibility for my actions.

The group commander showed no mercy on that particular run. I had a responsibility to the unit. Regardless of how much pain I was in, I was expected to fulfill my duties. The noncommissioned officer in charge realized I could barely hold the pace of the run. He tried to encourage me as the pace of the run quickened. Finally, the run was finished, and the group commander dismissed the formation.

However, my tail was still in trouble. The company commander was about to have a piece of me, no matter what I said. She came over to me with a look of anger, but empathy in her voice. She knew what had happened. Without sounding overly sympathetic, she proceeded to chew me out. I just looked at her. My tail was already thin from so many ass-chewings that day already, that one more from a senior-ranking officer was not going to faze me. She closed out her remarks by saying, "Son, you are in the military now, so you had better damn well start acting like it."

Well, I could have said, "I just discovered I was bipolar last night," but I didn't know that for sure, and neither did anybody else. I had a hunch that my life was not going to be very fruitful from then on. I looked at her rather complacently and realized she was very serious. "Damn my soul for getting myself into this position," I thought.

The post-concussion aching continued in the right hemisphere of my brain, causing pain that drove me to the local medical treatment facility at SHAPE (Supreme Headquarters Allied Powers Europe, Belgium). I knew the specialist in charge of the ER. She could see almost instantaneously that I was gripped by pain of an unknown origin and maybe some other forces she had never encountered before. She whispered in my ear, trying to calm my fears, but I think that was beyond her beautiful voice that day. The doctor who was on duty was a full bird colonel who barely glanced over me. The only thing I recall is that he insulted my integrity by implying I was avoiding my military duty. My anger nearly exploded. This man clearly didn't understand that the right hemisphere of my brain was on fire. I had a profound fear of the unknown as to what might happen if things went catastrophic. I cried as I left the emergency room. Lisa followed me out in silence, sensing the pain I was in. I knew I had to somehow deal with this issue on a proactive basis in order to survive.

After the examination in the Emergency Room was finished, the group commander wanted me to handle troop-oriented details, in order to sharpen my basic leadership skills and to give me a chance to catch up to other company grade officers with similar types of duties. I was appointed the Executive Officer of the Headquarters Company. I thought a change of assigned duties would help me sharpen my leadership skills and decrease the amount of time I spent self-medicating. Initially, to some extent, it did. But in the long run it did not. The concussion syndrome intensified, especially when the unit went to the local indoor range and my glaucoma grew more intense when I tried to qualify by myself. I was never going to qualify at that point in time, unless an act of God interfered by throwing rocks at my targets. Between my headaches and my eyes, I prayed that somehow things would resolve themselves.

My pain was not meant to stop there, it seems. For some reason, the headquarters company commander had decided to enter a team from our unit into the 21st TAACOM Military Stakes Competition. She picked me to be the officer in charge of the team. I just hung my head when I found out. I was wondering if the chain of command was trying to punish me for the mistakes I had made six months before. What depressed me even more was that I didn't even realize at that point in my life what it was like to be a true leader. Right then I could only focus on my post-concussion pain. It was going to take every ounce of energy I could muster to pull this off.

The training started in the deep humidity of the summer. I had a chance to work with some of the finest soldiers stationed in the nation of Belgium, but I simply couldn't concentrate on putting myself in the role of the leader, due to the severity of the post-concussion pain I was in. So until I learned better, I was just content to be one of the followers. However, when I was trained to standard, I quickly became the leader I wanted to be. When it came to physical training, I took a back seat to none of my team members. I still couldn't qualify with my rifle, but I could assemble and disassemble a machine gun blindfolded in less than a minute, which was no small consolation for not being able to qualify in marksmanship.

Finally, it was time to travel to Germany for the competition. The most painful thing I can recall about the competition in Germany was the physical fitness test. When I saw the two-mile course, I knew it was going to test my physical limitations, but I had trained extremely hard and was determined to conquer the mountainside. My non-commissioned officer in charge challenged me to participate on the spot. I thought to myself, "Why am I putting myself through so much agony?" However, it became an obsession for me to finish the run and prove I was worthy of being the leader. I do wish, though, I had taken a handful of aspirin before charging down the mountain so impulsively. I was either extremely competitive or borderline obsessive-compulsive. I finished the run in ten minutes flat, which was a personal best for me, but with pain shooting out my eyes. I wondered why I was torturing myself that way.

People with the bipolar illness are sometimes noted to have abnormal sexual behavior. I was no exception to this. I thrived on the red-light districts outside of Brussels. This was a behavior pattern that not even my Commander expected. The first time I went to a red-light bar, I thought I was going for a drink with the boys. I was a country boy who was high on life and champagne, which led only to a desirable Belgian woman. This opened up a side of life I really didn't want to experience just then. My reputation was hanging in the balance, but at that point, I really didn't care. To my chagrin, this turned into a repetitive affair on a weekly basis.

Up to this point I had tried everything to deal with the insanity of my life and what it would take to turn my life around. The only thing that made sense was to drink insanely. I was extremely upset with myself about that decision and about the poor leader I was turning out to be.

I was confused about how things in my military career had gone astray so quickly. I was extremely hesitant to go back to old habits in which I had found some peace of mind. The habits had stimulated me, such as weight lifting, but I was afraid of hurting myself due to poor concentration. It seemed as if others in my cohort like Kim really knew what was going on in their careers. Nobody had really taken time to analyze my problems, and since the medical opinions from the local military hospital had failed to turn up anything, everybody assumed there was nothing wrong. However, that was about to change quickly with the local Change of Command ceremony.

I had been in Belgium for approximately ten months when the first change of command came about. By then my time in the office had taken a downward spiral. I was dating the most beautiful female enlisted service member I had ever known, which was the last thing my new Commanding Officer expected of his adjutant. Her strawberry-blonde hair was like no other woman's that I had been with in the past. Her lean and tight body was pressed hard to my muscular frame every morning. Yet from time to time I would still stray off into my foolish habits of previous months. Medically, I was going downhill rapidly. My post-concussion syndrome was running wild through the right hemisphere of my brain. The glaucoma in my eyes was burning, plus I was noted for being excessively generous in monetary affairs. Manic-depressives are typically spendthrifts when on a high.

I was really unsure about what I had gotten myself into. For the past ten months I had been aggressively harassed by a field-grade staff of lieutenant colonels, where there had been little fair play. I was just a young lad then. My efforts to help my boss were endless. He treated me as if he were a father figure to me when I proved my loyalty and commitment to him, despite my rocky start at the beginning of my military tour in Belgium. Between the future conflicts with Kuwait and Iraq and the ever-increasing irrational behavior I was exhibiting, I knew it was time for me to resign. My commander thought I was making a mistake; he would not concur with my resignation, but I didn't have any more resilience at that time. However, until my resignation became official from the Department of Defense, the unit had a mission and so did I.

The Colonel tasked my boss, the Director of Personnel and Community Activities (the DPCA), with developing a staffing project for managing the staff of the NATO/SHAPE Support Group. I was the focal person for writing this document. When I received the assignment, I could barely snap a salute to the DPCA to acknowledge that I understood what was expected of me. I just rolled my eyes and left his office with pain ringing in my head.

I had never considered myself an alcoholic up to this point, but it was killing me not to have some sort of relief. Whether it was the Officers'

Club or the club at the airbase, I was there every night to drown my sorrows. The pain in my eyes consistently irritated me, which the enlisted soldiers who worked for me tried to understand. Those enlisted soldiers took me under their wing, because for the first time in ten months my leadership could not be counted on. One of my NCO's asked me why I let my boss treat me so poorly. I thought your boss was a father figure to you. I told her I was following orders, and until my new boss had more faith in my abilities, I would do my best to stand on my two feet. My boss was training me on the skills and arts of becoming a highly skilled AG officer, but I hated him for his ignorance about my medical problems, which I had tried to openly and directly explain to him.

There is a dangerous borderline between knowledge and ignorance, which was evident in this scenario. I had so much indirect anger at both the DPCA and the 21st Personnel Group Commander that I knew I was going to fail the mission of writing the project, due to my pain and agony.

When I was able to put my pain aside, I used thought-processes professionally as a true gentleman. Taking on the challenge would be appropriate. However, I also had to deal with the glaucoma and the bipolar disorder, which no one knew I had. This affected my ability to make clear and concise decisions from that moment forward.

The next day was the beginning of the end for me in Belgium. My internal demons were about to be unleashed. I was mentally exhausted from the previous night and I was also ready to break down in tears, which characterized the bipolar illness. The drinking, adjusted workload, and lack of medical attention had driven me to the edge. Finally, I left my office and went down to the company commander's office, where I had a nervous breakdown. I took a chair into one of the back offices and cried my eyes out for two hours, hating life for what it had done to me.

The Army's decision had already been made for me to go to Germany and maybe even the warfront, but the decision-makers had no idea of the injuries I had suffered and the mental abuse I had taken while being subservient to six field-grade officers. Tear after tear ran down my cheek. I was embarrassed that a man of my position and stature was crying. I was going to Germany to a unit that was packed to deploy and which was directly supporting units that were deploying. I was about to embark on a whole new journey that I hoped would find the cure for my illnesses. My thoughts were frozen every night, as I was praying for a solution to the problems that had plagued me for almost a year in Belgium.

Within forty-eight hours of receiving instructions from the Department of the Army, I received my marching orders to pack up and move to

Germany on a no-cost move. I felt confident about the move, but I really didn't know what I was getting into. It would turn into an ordeal I never expected. It took me two weeks to get to Germany when I reported to my command. I thought I made a positive impression when I met my Commander for the first time except for the mild swings I was experiencing. But the swings didn't scare me: my commander had confidence in me. It was only the demon in me that would turn my life into complete chaos. I wish it had not been that way, but it was.

The mood swings energized me to the point of personal destruction. I was hurting myself. The intensity and drama of Desert Storm picked up, and so did I. My personal insanity would not keep me from accomplishing my mission and getting my promotion. However, the Commander thought I was going to burn out my troops and therefore he pulled in my manic leash. My aggressiveness started to burn me out, and my mood swings were more apparent all the time. I had the most incredible urge to drive myself to a whole new level. I had a real-world mission. My reputation of being a first-rate AG officer was on the line, and I would not be denied. However, my negative behavior from Belgium caught up with me and once again I was burning the candle at both ends. My misbehavior was becoming more apparent by the moment. Already I had begun to get the suspicion that various soldiers were complaining to the Commander about my personal life. With the preparation for a field training exercise to see how we could perform in a tactical environment, my downfall was about to come.

I thought I could prepare myself for any intellectual occasion, but my brain was not cycling information correctly. I had pulled the most stupendous tactical move an officer could ever pull. I thought I was slick enough to withdraw my weapon early for a field training exercise and not return it to the arms room at close of business that day. But the Commander caught me dead to rights, and I had no justification as to why there was an unsecured weapon in my office. I was finished and I knew it. I made no excuse for my actions, but just shook my head in shame. The pressure was building up inside me. I felt the negativity growing inside me, knowing that each new day would bring me closer to my demise in the Army. My negative energy was becoming incredibly apparent all the time. My commander tried to counsel me about my poor performance on the unit's field training exercise, but I knew I was finished.

My nonchalant behavior was taking place outside the office as well. As in Belgium, I also lacked a vehicle. The way I went about trying to get one could have gotten me relieved of duty if anyone had apprehended me in the process. Since I needed to go to the local medical treatment facility one day, I took a Ranger pickup truck for a test drive. Ninety minutes later, I got back to the dealership and found out the dealership was ready to call the Military Police. I don't know why my Commander stepped in for me on that occasion, but he did. However, the pain in my head ricocheted to no end, and I knew it was only a matter of time until my days in Germany would come to an end. Why my commander continually gave me the benefit of the doubt, I will never know. I knew I was in for a lasting experience while I was in Germany; I just didn't know how bad the price to be paid was going to be. Only then did I realize that the commander was trying to become involved with my treatment for legitimate reasons.

I had to report back to the local hospital the following morning. This time my commanding officer was breathing down my neck to give me my marching instructions. I took the military bus there with my head pounding. I was not very confident that the local hospital could do anything for me.

This was a time of suffering I would recall for many days to come. I tried to sleep on the bus, but every little rattle made my head vibrate back and forth. I made it to the hospital without any more undue pain. I didn't know what to expect from the doctor's analysis or what to ask of him. By this time, I had given up all hope the pain in the right hemisphere of my brain would be going away. On the ride back to the company, I had so much pain from my concussion that I had to convince the bus driver to pull over, so I could find the nearest bush to crawl behind and vomit. This was not how I envisioned my career in Germany would end.

Oddly enough, in my battered state the issue of weapons qualification came up again. I didn't put up an argument anymore. The Commander knew I was a broken man and he was going to put nails in my coffin. I had not qualified since I had been in Germany. Just to show the world what a lousy marksman I truly was, he was going to let one of our sister units evaluate me. I had no energy for such a task; my head rang out in pain at every possible moment.

I went to the range and found a place in the sun to take a nap until it was my turn to fire. At that point I had no desire to do anything else. I blew off ten rounds, then went back to napping because the concussion rang so intensely in my head. I was in so much pain I asked about the possibility of checking into the Lanstuhl Hospital a week early. Well, Commanders talk to Commanders, so I was thoroughly in the shit house when I got back to the company area that afternoon. But I was mentally exhausted, and I really didn't care. I just wanted to hit the Officers' Club and drink it off. The commanding officer didn't really care from that point forward, either. He saw me as a pain in the neck, and he was looking for an easy way to get rid of me without actually understanding why. The day of reckoning was about to happen.

I walked down the hallway to the Commanding Officer and requested permission to enter. Within seconds, I went into a manic-depressive mood swing and broke down in tears. My commander must have been doing his homework up to that point, because the next thing I knew, I was on a three-day psychiatric stay in the Landstuhl Army Medical Facility. I stammered and stuttered, trying to explain what I was feeling to my commander, but my efforts did not prevail. I had never asked to be this way. Even though I could see the anger in my boss's eyes, I could also see how much he understood.

I had done everything possible to help the unit survive Operation Golden Python and had elevated my performance to an all-time high, but eventually my efforts were in vain. My dreams of becoming a field grade officer were over. I didn't understand clinical experimentation at that point. It just seemed as if things were going to roll that way for a long time to come. I have personal feelings about the whole thing, but right then I felt they were kind of irrelevant, because I probably didn't have the education or ability to apply myself to properly ascertain the situation. Perhaps my pain and suffering could have been better avoided if I had been more enlightened.

I loved my uniform and I loved what I had been tasked to do, but at the same I could not bear the onslaught of the pain my body and mind were being put through. When I was admitted to Landstuhl I was given a psychiatric evaluation and started on a new medication called Tegretol. I didn't know what the medication was in a pharmaceutical sense, but I would soon see how it tempered my mood swings. My unit commander was tasked with getting my personal effects together. The last time I saw him was when he brought my uniform to my hospital room and left me with a nice little compliment, saying I was messed up in the head. I thought that would be a rather rough memory to dwell on. In fact, it does surface from time to time. It makes me wonder if war actually has to be that cruel. I guess it must have been, for better or for worse.

It took an incredible effort to deal with the ups and downs of the bipolar illness while I was in Europe, plus all the negative attributes that are associated with the illness. I found myself constantly trapped by the bipolar illness. I am purely disgusted by some of the atrocious things I did. I longed to be number one among company grade AG officers, but my mind was trapped at every corner. I could not cope with stress as quickly as my peers. Even on a social level, my life had started to fall apart. The Commander was having a unit dinner on a fall evening. I wondered if I could compose myself and maintain my decorum throughout the ceremony. By the time dinner started, I had composed myself, only to be foolish enough to have a beer or two, which probably set me off again. I took a seat with one of my warrant officers, who took it upon himself to be my guardian angel for the evening (Thanks, Henry, for bailing me out of a tight one that night). I couldn't keep my big mouth shut. With one quick psychiatric outburst, I put all my pain on him that evening. I had suffered so much psychiatric damage from the past that I wasn't sure if I knew how to handle myself anymore. I had been punished to the uttermost extreme by my previous Commander.

My biggest problem is that I think I have to blame myself as much as anybody else for everything that has happened in the past. There are a lot of choice words I could think of right now, but I still remember I am a commissioned officer and I need to maintain my decorum, especially now that I am stable and people look to me for leadership more than anything.

I would be in the Landstuhl Hospital from three to five days with a preliminary diagnosis of post-concussion syndrome, which didn't tell me anything I didn't already know. I also knew that a lot of senior-ranking officers, such as the one I had encountered at SHAPE, didn't know what it meant, either. My anger still haunts me to this day that the Emergency Room doctor made the rash judgment he did. Kind of like I did that haunted night on the Belgium landscape. It took a year of suffering and misery to finally get the attention I needed. It was time I quit being a hero and did everything possible to get my life back. I was administered every psychiatric and psychological test in the book, yet for some reason I still felt like I was avoiding responsibility. I didn't understand what bipolar disorder was, and nobody was giving me the information I needed to give myself a fighting chance to overcome it. I knew I had a mental problem, but no one could define for me exactly what the problem was. After being in the hospital for approximately two or three days, I started to feel light and loopy. The decision was made to send me back to the States that very weekend. I was started on an antidepressant to get ready for the flight home. Depression was an endless feeling at that time.

When I had a scheduled departure date out of Ramstein Air Force Base on a C-130, I was placed on Tegretol and an antidepressant to calm me before the flight.

My ability to focus was incomplete. I had a kind spirit in which I wanted to help everybody, even though I was completely incapable of doing so. Out of the corner of my eye I saw two airmen conversing about what I assumed was my medication. Out of pure curiosity I edged closer to them and tried to listen in on their conversation. I could clearly hear what they were saying and felt I could help solve their problems. I don't think they understood what I was trying to do, and I also don't think they really cared. Between the two of them, they kindly escorted me back to my seat and made me very aware that I was not to leave my seat at any point. To make sure I understood their instructions, the flight physician gave me another Tegretol. I didn't wake up until the flight touched down at Dulles. When the rear door opened, there was the largest heat blast that had ever hit me and it was incredible. I had never been so happy to be on American soil. I gently kissed the ground I stepped on, then picked myself up like a real man and walked to the hospital shuttle, not knowing what I was getting myself into from then on. Previously, I had lived for every ounce of energy I had spent in winning my gold bar, but something told me I was on the verge of losing it. Down deep inside as I waited in the reception area, I knew this was it.

After ten minutes of meandering in the reception lounge, my fellow veterans and I were taken to the Walter Reed Army Medical Center. However, the only thing that mattered to me right then was the incessant pounding in my head. It just wouldn't go away. I leaned my head forward against the seat in front of me and prayed for just one ounce of mercy, but I knew none would be forthcoming.

The shuttle bus unloaded at the hospital, and I was ushered into the psychiatric part of the hospital. When I approached the ward that I was going to be a part of, I asked what kind of unit I was being placed in. The nurse's reply was, "The post-concussion lock-down and observation ward." If they had had any other serious theories about what my diagnosis was, they would have been able to spend more time diagnosing the problem from there on out. But I had so much pain in my head right then that any means of analyzing my injury sounded great to me. There continued to be no direct diagnosis that I was bipolar at that point in time.

My first night on the ward felt like a direct punishment. I sat in the hallway outside of my room and cried as I clenched my uniform. I tried to convince myself I was going back to active duty, but my tears were in vain. My tears were real and not as phony as the staff may have thought they were. I didn't even have to consult the medical staff to realize that my days of being a bull in a china shop were over and I would not be returning to active duty.

My first true love in life was over. The crying continued. Quietly I hung my uniform in my closet and never found it again. I finally gave up on having any future career in the Army. I was asked time and time again to stay in the Army, which was like asking me to make an analytical decision without numbers and data. I felt like my intelligence was being insulted repeatedly, because I was constantly bombarded with negative thoughts. Medical staff members continually asked me if I wanted to go back on active duty. It was like trying to make a command decision without input or feedback from any staff members. In this particular case, I really didn't want to make a decision based on the input I was receiving. I thought the input was inadequate.

It was just one psychiatric test after another. I could hardly bear the insults to my intelligence. I felt I was beyond the stage of being constantly belittled. I cried myself to sleep every night, wondering why the staff couldn't do more to help me with the mental anguish I was experiencing. I could not even begin to fathom what my mental issues were just then, and I didn't even know then if I was bipolar or not. If I was bipolar, I was either in too much pain to understand or the medical staff was not very direct in explaining it to me. Every time I tried to ask about the issues that affected me, I felt like I was talking in vain. I was looking for a short and well- clarified answer, which never came. My soul was constantly under fire.

I was noted for being able to manage irregular financial situations when I was in the military. I should have been noted for just being irresponsible and somewhat fiscally stupid. I had a relative who had a business, and that business seemed to be floundering when I went in the military. So I took it upon myself to spot that relative an unusually large amount of money to the point where it fiscally hurt me. I thought this relative would justifiably treat me with the same kindness that I treated them and create a job for me after I left Walter Reed. Well the job lasted for about six months and the hatred with the relative lasted for half of a lifetime. The whole idea is to let bygones be bygones, and eventually it gets to the point where that is the case, but you never forget and by 1992 my memory had been scorched thoroughly. So, by 1992, my thoughts on dominating a local business scene were given up, and I moved back home. Damn myself for being so gullible. In 1990, it sounded like an awesome idea, but I knew nothing about the downsides of loaning people money without seeking the aid of a lawyer. I always wondered how many times I was going to let people take advantage of me because I was a kind-hearted soul and I didn't know when to quit turning the other cheek. From 1992 to 1994 I was living at home. I didn't fully understand what my medical issues were at that point in time even though a psychiatrist at the Lebanon VAMC tried to explain to me that I was bipolar. I don't remember studying that one in psychology or perhaps I was just too hung over to notice at the time. Things were at the point where I really didn't care anymore. I didn't care where I was working as long as I could afford to pay the rent and I had a roof over my head. I have to really apologize to my parents because they were stuck with taking care of me even though I worked in other businesses than the family business. I was tired of the ups and downs and trying to deal with the excuses I could create for myself because I didn't understand what was wrong. I enjoyed my side excursions to the Lebanon VAMC to get out of work and somehow foster my own personal knowledge. Great, I thought. I am here, I am bipolar, now what is somebody else teaching me about it? My psychiatrist and I had the most enlightening conversations and we started to develop a strong relationship based on the intellectual bond that we established. I grew as an academician and a true leader under his tutelage. My thirst for knowledge continued to expand and drive me forward to go back to college in 1994 at Lebanon Valley College.

My decision to return to Lebanon Valley College during this time period left me emotionally charged. The Veteran's Administration offered to send me back to school on a Chapter 31 scholarship to pursue a degree in Business Management. My thoughts, contrary to getting a degree in Management, were to get a degree in secondary education social studies and be a soccer coach. Talking about thinking rather on the lofty side. The VA had me quickly adjust my way of thinking to theirs, otherwise I would have to forego my scholarship. Needless to say, I didn't challenge the government like I did in ROTC and decided their way of thinking might be best. Ironically, Dr. Barney Raddfield became my class advisor and he went on to teach my first class in Marketing. Making poor decisions was an issue that I struggled with for years to come. I was stunned with the outcome of my first grade in Marketing when I got a D for the grade and I had a hard time explaining to my VA academic advisor as to why my first cumulative GPA for the marking period was below a 2.0. For some reason I told myself that I needed balance outside of school to give me more focus and awareness of what the real world was all about. So, I went out and got a girlfriend, a good job by Lancaster standards, and I moved away from home. I think all my decisions were solid except for the girlfriend. I don't know what I was thinking there. She was cute, and I thought she was helping me improve. It just turned out that for some reason she didn't like the way I was. Clearly, there were going to be consequences for my rash behavior of bringing her into my life. The relationship we had would prove to be damaging in the long run as our feelings for each other become borderline hostile on many occasions.

As the journey continued I was beginning to wonder if my trail of tears would ever end. After losing my job again thanks to an overzealous boss, I went to the VA again where my doctor got me level one more time, only to have the evil wench of a girlfriend manipulate me one last time. I was her little experiment. She twisted my emotions and said if I truly loved her I would try and come off of my medications for her. She kept on harping on the issue until I caved and gave her my undying love and then told her she was probably going to be in for one hell of a ride. She also had the audacity to tell me it was socially acceptable in her eyes for me to drink while I was out with her. We were engaged at the time and I had the gut feeling that this proclamation on her behalf was going to be the one that broke the camel's back and ended our relationship once and for all. I don't know what I was thinking at the time. Maybe my next thoughts will explain it.

She swore she would never try to hurt me. I told myself that I was so madly in love with her that I believed her. I ignored my mother's repeated advice on many occasions. I wanted her to be for me. The next step seemed so small a step to take. We were on the verge of being engaged to be married and it seemed like her perfectionist motivations to improve me were meant for us, but little did I know my pain was no objective. She knew I was bipolar and on medication and at the time I felt great. My mistake was that I truly loved her. I couldn't imagine she would do anything to disrupt the happiness that I thought we had between us. Why she had a level of contempt for me I will never know, but for some reason she was going to attempt to mold me in her image no matter what it cost me. I loved Joan enough that I let her do as she wished, even though I knew that what she was doing was wrong and would only harm me in the long run. I tried to believe that she did love me and that somehow if she was trying to wrong me, it was possible that she would do so out of love.

Maybe I was just being paranoid at this point in time, but I trusted her and I gave into her little scheme and started phasing off of my medication. I was never any more of the fool than I was at that moment. I didn't tell a soul what I was doing and my psychiatrist didn't catch on right away because I skipped my blood tests. That was the first major mistake that I could have made. I think that when he figured out what I did, he decided to let me learn my mistake the hard way. I could have saved myself so much misery by not letting Joan lord over me and be such a push over. My rationale was that I loved her and it was acceptable to do blind and irrational things when in love. My critical thinking has become quite sharper as an adult than it was a decade and a half ago. I haven't been in love since either.

After that, I started doing blind and stupid things to overcompensate and please my loved one. Everything I did was over and beyond my capacity of handling, but that fact had no real bearing upon me at that point in time because everything I did was for my beloved. I didn't feel like I was off my medication. If anything, I felt kind of euphoric and pleased with myself, like I had moved to a whole new plateau in personal development. I just wanted to satisfy my dear lady no matter what and she was playing on my sympathies to the maximum. I was so blindly in love with her that I could not see the obvious signs of relapse when they were about to occur right in front of me. The only person that was going to suffer was myself and I was acting like I didn't care because I was with my beloved. When would I learn?

No matter what the situation, Joan and I could never find peace of mind between us. Joan and I went out to dinner one night and I tried to have a civil conversation, except I was charged and devastated and on the verge of crying. Joan just thought I was being emotional and overly sensitive and since I was her first illogical boyfriend I was never in tune with her conversations. Little did she know I was having a hypomanic spell caused by the woman I loved because I let her manipulate me into being what she wanted me to be. Having a beer at dinner that night did not do anything to help matters either. To add insult to injury, my dear Joan had the audacity to criticize me on how ill-mannered I was at dinner that evening and it was only socially acceptable for me to treat myself to a beer at dinner and I needed to learn how to handle it better. Imagine after ten years of being bipolar, I would have known better than to have a beer anywhere. This is not only socially unacceptable, but it is like putting a nail in your own coffin...

Then the madness and the insanity all began when I switched jobs to work for a local manufacturer doing inside sales. I had a passion and a desire for my new job from the get go. I don't know if either one of my bosses detected my passion, but my future fiancé did from the beginning and it drove her crazy. Joan could not handle me going in early to work or staying late or not fearing to drive like a madman to make it down to Philadelphia to attend my MBA classes at LaSalle University at least twice a week. The drive alone was pure insanity, but I loved what I was doing and I would not be denied. I was obsessed with it, but somehow I could sense it was my future and down deep I would not be denied. Since I was also denying myself my medication it was only a matter of time till I was either hypomanic or depressed to some extent. Amazingly enough, Joan would punish me on that issue. Before I knew it, we were getting couples counseling from a Catholic priest. She declared her love for me and I should have gagged on the spot except I was having a hypomanic seizure at the time. I was very concerned about my job, and my boss was concerned about my ability to do my job. I wanted to say I would not be denied, but the end result was inevitable and any potential I had with the inside sales team of that manufacturer was quickly flushed down the tubes.

As my personal saga at that job came to an end, so did my ability to think rationally for a time. My thinking was up and down and I was very distraught. I was constantly stressed. Joan wanted to move closer to her parents and I was wondering what was wrong with her existing economic condition. Upfront, she was in a very enviable position, but according to her she had to move anyway, and it only took her a matter of a few weeks to sell her beautiful colonial and buy a three-bedroom house with a two-car garage. Needless to say, only one car was going to go in that garage, and it wasn't mine. Also, I wasn't on medication, so there was always the chance of manic behavior; for example, due to overexertion from loading her moving van. I got Joan's van loaded with the help of a friend one evening and I drove it to her house the following morning. My mission according to Joan was to unload the van in one-hundred-degree weather with no water while she and her parents went to make settlement on the house. In three hours with no water I unloaded two thirds of the van. I just drove myself on and on like there was no tomorrow. At this point I was ready to tell Joan that the relationship was over because she really didn't realize what I was doing for her. I hated her more than ever for allowing myself to be put in a position where they could put me in a much worse position than what I deserved to be in. She came back to the van and applauded my efforts with a big kiss and like a fool I let her smooth over my ruffled feathers and keep on driving me hard to help her family for the rest of the afternoon. The thing about it was there was not a member of her family that took a kindred spirit towards me no matter what I did, no matter how hard I tried. I got more of a response from Joan's mom when I would dance with Joan at the country club and we would perhaps snuggle a little bit too closely. I don't see what she was worried about, I really wasn't a great dancer. Perhaps her mother was more concerned about the fact that I might order another steak or something and she would have to pay for it. That woman was incredibly tight on money (and my mother gets on me about such issues seventeen years later!).

The day ended with every muscle in my body aching. My thoughts and my heart told me to hate her, but deep inside I couldn't, because she was my future wife and I was a man of honor. I was beginning to slowly realize that she was deliberately abusing me, but it had not dawned upon me that she had won this victory over me by swaying me to go off medication. I was so gullible at that point in my life. I would have even openly admitted that I was stupid and naïve for allowing this woman to do what she did to me, however that is exactly what I let happen. Her little manipulation to turn me into her personal slave had nearly driven my sanity over the edge. My degree, my job, my loyalty to my friends, and my personal self-worth all meant nothing at this point. I needed to regain my self-respect and prove to the world once again that I was the man I claimed myself to be. But deep down inside, no matter how much I wanted that to happen, I knew that wasn't going to be easy. To this day, I still know nothing but hatred for how easily my love for a woman allowed me to be manipulated.

Shortly after the whole moving affair, life as I knew it began to move downhill once again and I realized my dearly beloved was doing anything she could possibly do to drive me into the ground without question. I turned to the world of information technology to try and solve my woes. I started with America On Line and I fell prey to the chat rooms very quickly. However, for some idiotic reason I was so loyal to my dear Joan that when I did meet the desirable angel that might prove to be a future part of me, I just drove up my phone bill chatting with her. I was quite the fool not to seek her company because she openly wanted mine, but I was so fearful of my bipolar side that I would not venture in that direction. Joan became knowledge of my phone calls to this young princess when I was naïve enough to share a phone bill with her. Our relationship was never the same after that. I never really learned to be discrete about anything when it came to Joan. This woman really had my head spinning and unfortunately, I was about to pay a heavy price until I recognized my freedom.

From that time forward, it was nothing but one argument after the next. We would go to parties and there was ice between us the whole night. Why I was obsessed in proving that I could make this relationship work with Joan was beyond me. I had come to realize that she didn't love me, but I was the fool in our relationship and she knew it. She said I was jealous of her because she had resources and I didn't. I had issues holding jobs bought on by manic behavior which allowed her to cause in me. Of course, she had resources, and I didn't! I had been manic free for five years now and the tide had turned. She was setting me up to become dependent on her except I would not allow myself to be completely susceptible to the level. We went through some serious ups and downs at that point. One night we arrived back at my apartment and we were having a very heated debate. It was quite dark out. She threatened to take her ring and throw it off into my driveway. I made it really clear to her at that point that if she took the ring off and threw it at me we were finished. I think she took me really seriously that evening, because her ring never did come off until another night when we broke up and she threw it back at me. Like I promised to her, she never got the ring back. It gave me some valuable pocket money to restart my life after I left the Philadelphia area. I was very foolish. I recall the moment I purchased her ring for her and how big of a fool I was for doing that.

It was Saturday morning and somehow Joan knew exactly how much money I had in my checking account. Normally, I had no problem going shopping with her, but I had a sick feeling this morning. I had been out pricing rings and for some reason I think Joan had been out doing the same. I was clearly left with the impression that my choice of rings for my dear lady was not good enough for her because we only went to one jewelry store and that is the one that she chose for us to go to. It was a cute little store on Main Street and we spent about an hour in the store. If I was not an expert on ring clarity going into the store, I was when

I came out. I let Joan have her wishes and oddly enough her wishes cost $6,200! Joan and I had a spat about that financial decision later on in the week, but she said "if you truly love me, you'll make our relationship complete by buying this ring." What a fool I was...it worked on me anyway. I was awesome at falling for Joan's emotional lines of bull. It always worked on me. I was beginning to think she worked every angle to make my life miserable.

Thinking back, it was our big night and the sky was filled with stars. I had not been to a country club in the longest period of time. The Round Circle Country Club was the *prima donna* country club in all of Lancaster County and Joan and I had been invited there for a night full of festivities. Being the ultimate conservative and tight-wad, I thought this would be my night to rise to the occasion and propose. I think Joan was kind of expecting it though. The club was the most fabulous I had ever been to, even compared to the fabulous officer's club at SHAPE, Belgium. The meals were paid for, free valet parking, and the only thing that was missing was my nine-iron to go out and try the driving range. Rule for all bipolars: just because you have a few at the club while you're off medication does not give you permission to do what I did at that point in my life. What I did was a big mistake. Think twice before you act when it comes to your health. I was thinking in Joan's world at that point in time and not in the world of my medical treatment team. I was a nervous fool that evening and I was not thinking clearly from the get go. Twenty years have lapsed since that evening and I can assure anyone that reads this book that even though I loved this woman with all my heart I have matured in my own way and not her way and I live my life for what is right for me today.

Well, the clock struck midnight in the ballroom and I was full of adrenaline and excitement. It was my time to shine for my heavenly angel or my misperception of an angel. I had noticed a side-sitting room with a gas fireplace when we had entered the club, on the other side of the receiving area. I proceeded to that room and asked the attendants if they could round up my dear fiancé. All the girls looked at me quizzically, so I pulled the ring out of my jacket and they all let out a gasp. I was like great, give it away, like Joan didn't know, but at least allow me to be a gentleman and go through the motions. I seated myself in the room while one of the attendants went out to round up my slightly intoxicated angel. Joan came back and just looked at me in a quizzical fashion. It was like the festivities of the evening had helped her forget I was carrying a one carat diamond in my jacket. I got down on one knee and kind of, well sort of, proposed to her.

She just sat there stunned and looked me in the eyes for a second. I was like "well, what is your decision?" It was like she was trying to cross-examine me on such a simple question. Then she spoke up. "Are you sure you want to do this?" I looked at her in a completely quizzical fashion and wondered what in tarnation she was asking me. It didn't make sense. I had just proposed to her with a diamond she picked out and I paid cash for and she wants to know if I want to marry her! Guys, if you ever run into this situation, no matter how much you love her, pack it in and run for the hills. Use the resale value of the ring as collateral to restart your life. I wish I would have followed my own advice. Welcome to three years of purgatory. I would never see balance in my life again until 2004 no matter how hard I worked and no matter what I did professionally. To make a long story short, Joan and I went our separate directions in roughly 1999. She dragged me to court that year down in Montgomery County for violating a restraining order which she didn't have a leg to stand on. My lawyer represented me very well and Joan lost her case hands down. I haven't seen her since. I am smiling as I relive the thoughts of seeing her in court. It was an expensive relief not to have to see her in my life anymore.

One of the things that I really despise doing is reflecting back on all the negatives of being bipolar and trying to correct them. I have discovered that one of the side effects of being bipolar is that you can be very narcissistic. I am very extreme when it comes to narcissism. Narcissistic traits can be associated with a personality disorder in which the person has a distorted self-image, is unstable, and has intense emotions. There are many times in which I may have been overly preoccupied with vanity, a false sense of prestige, power, and yet a feeling a personal inadequacy. These tendencies were often especially present if my illness was presenting itself: exaggerated by me being slightly manic at times. There were times when I really lacked empathy towards other people, and I had an exaggerated sense of superiority. I really hated myself for being that shallow of a person, and that experience gives me all the more of an incentive to stay on medication. There were times when I really didn't care about other people's feelings, and over time, these traits were intensified by PTSD or the bipolar illness. Making me feel more inadequate about myself in the long run. As I write this, I wonder how I could have been so socially inept, but it is part of my personal treatment plan to work at my social skills.

As I was going through my growing pains in college, (even though I was not a hundred percent sure because I had not been labeled as being bipolar at the time) I felt like I had experienced self-love traits on a periodic basis. Mind you, this is only a hypothesis. I had to boost my own ego by enrolling in all the top classes which for some ill begotten reason made me feel intellectually superior to all my classmates, when my neuro-psych evaluations say otherwise (Keep on writing books, dummy). To my chagrin, within two semesters, I had dropped all these advanced classes to pursue a more leisurely liberal arts program in History. I am not going out on a limb here and saying that this was a fluff major, but it didn't avail me the same opportunities that Analysis or Chemistry would have if I would have harnessed my energies and chose to excel. However, I had made a decision to apply myself and compete for an ROTC (Reserve Officer's Training Corp) Scholarship, and History degrees were in high demand at that point. Now that I sit here and reflect about how egotistical I was when I took Analysis and Chemistry at the same time, I wonder if it was possible that I might have been slightly hypomanic and the methods for identifying people with psychiatric difficulties really didn't measure up to the task or I was so socially inept that everybody just blew off my behavior as someone that really wasn't with it. However, despite what other people thought at that point in my life, I got into the Army as a commissioned officer, and even though it didn't last long, my second career choice as a professional writer is allowing me to pick up where I left off twenty-two years ago.

The Beginning of the End

The first thing to remember is that my illness had not manifested itself, while I was in ROTC. The professional officers constantly grooming me couldn't detect the illness. They couldn't detect it, or if they did, they didn't say anything about me having an issue. In retrospect, I wonder if any of them knew what the bipolar illness was, even if they were Vietnam survivors. I think they might have been operating under a rather bold assumption that anybody that could graduate from basic training would be good to go in the ROTC program. Also, as far as they were concerned, they just saw a young cadet grow with every professional encounter they had with me (except for when I lost a compass on a field training exercise).

It became an obsession for me to improve to become the best cadet that I could be beyond question. There were times when I far excelled being the best. I never wasted an opportunity to make the Blue

Mountain Battalion look good in training and I strived to learn everything I could as to what the Army had to offer. I felt like I was becoming the ultimate at what I do and I felt completely confident that I would professionally excel in the future as a commissioned officer. I wasn't manic at the time, I felt confident that after three long years of training I would be all that I could be! Then I went to Advanced Camp at Ft. Bragg and my dream career turned into a disaster!

One of the toughest obstacles I ever had to overcome was self-medicating with alcohol. Why I chose to start drinking at the time I did was beyond me, I just knew I had the deepest craving for it and somehow I kept on going till I punished myself beyond question. I never drank before I went to college and I am not saying the pressures of college brought out that negative side in me, but it was a new experience. I was only nineteen and on my own when I went to my first party that completely caused me to unwind. I found out I had a devil inside of me and for some reason I liked the experience. I didn't even realize what I was doing to myself. It was a great feeling to have. But to abuse of the alcohol became the norm. Once down that path it was a night of chasing internal demons if I chose to abuse alcohol for the rest of the night.

As the bipolar illness began to erupt in my life, it laid the groundwork for enabling alcohol abuse even though I didn't realize it. Every time I had some type of mood swing, I escaped reality by drinking. I don't know if friends and family sensed there was something wrong or not, or if they thought my drinking was like everyone else's. When I was in Europe, I would be in a club night after night throwing money away thinking I was just reliving my college years when, in reality, I was just trying to escape an evil inside of me. I was destined for failure in the military. I could not admit to myself that I had an abusive lifestyle. I was extremely grandiose in my thinking. No challenge was too big or small. I knew I had issues at this point, but I was at a loss for rational thinking. My days were dominated by manic ups and downs and evenings were dominated by the insanity of self-medication.

I think the thing that really helped me pull it together for the short term after I left the Army was when a captain made me promise to quit drinking before I was discharged. My word was as good as gold and that is exactly what I did. Even though I made the attempt to find a new identity for myself when I first left the military, I struggled to find a professional life for myself. I just roamed from one factory to the next, while I waited for my chance to go back to school and retrain. In 1993, they told me I was bipolar and I didn't take this lightly. I found it hard to believe the diagnosis and I didn't take the initiative to go out and research what the implications of this illness were. Even if I would have, I don't think I would have believed my own research and I would have been in self-denial. I was totally rebellious at that point in in my life and I was constantly in the mood to be anti-social. My self-esteem was at an all-time low. My downward spiral almost drove me to the point where I conceivably thought of ending my life. My medication was not strong enough, and my head was left spinning every day. The end result was that I was hospitalized at the Lebanon VA Medical Center for a few weeks, where some intense psychotherapy boosted my morale and new medications were added to keep me level. This helped get my wits about me and give me some grit and determination to go back to school.

I gained employment at a local bank, York Bank & Trust, as a financial sales representative halfway through the completion of my degree. Unfortunately, the bipolar illness had to lift its ugly head one more time. Any little negative event would cause me to break out crying and I would hide in a back stockroom to hide my emotions. My boss was less than ideal. I had never been harassed by a woman before, but it was happening. She didn't understand why I emotionally shut her out during the workday, but I didn't know how to handle her overzealous behavior. To move events along, human resources dismissed her on grounds of harassment and other issues. Four months later, I decided to seek employment elsewhere because my bipolar illness was an issue for me again and I really didn't know how to explain to anybody in the corporate structure that this was the source of my trouble.

In the meantime, as far as employment was concerned, I obtained a position with a high-tech manufacturer as an inside sales account manager. This was another job in which I was not level-headed and things were not destined to work out with my employer or fellow co-workers. I didn't completely understand the symptoms of being bipolar. I liked my job, but a lot of people in the corporate structure were getting angered by my inability to deal with my professional and personal issues. Granted, this was almost twenty years ago, but my growing pains were tough even though, ironically, I did enjoy my job. The company showed faith in me when they gave me a degree of financial assistance towards my Master's degree. Unfortunately, the eruption of my bipolar temperament ruined the whole thing for me and my boss recognized that something was wrong. I don't know if she realized what the problem was, but she knew I had a problem and she probably made the best decisions for the company and for me that she could honestly make.

My professional life took me to the Philadelphia area where I thought I had found the dream job of my choice as a cost accountant. The salary was excellent, the benefits were awesome, and I had a good boss. The only thing that didn't work for my new boss was when he found out something was wrong with me. I tried everything to maintain professional decorum at work, but bipolars are excellent at being overly witty and, in my case, I had a really bad habit of bashing anybody that was intellectually inferior to me or slightly older. I was so good at doing that I really didn't pay attention to my own mental mistakes, which got me in even more hot water. As a cost accountant, it was my job to maintain accountability of the inventory from the time it came in the door, went into production, and out the door as a finished product. The business had some issues with their cash stream for a few months because my memory wasn't working very well at tracking inventory through their system. I won't blame this on anybody else because I could not multi-task while I was being slightly manicy. I came across well as a person, but in the corporate climate I was a wreck, and the controller was getting angry very quickly wondering why he had ever hired a MBA from my school. I didn't fault him for his decision to let me go after a certain period of time because, like him, I was an enlightened individual, and realized that I could have avoided many of these mistakes if I would have been taking better care of myself. My boss had a tough decision to make, but he made the right call. I survived and moved on. I don't fault him for something beyond his control or something he doesn't understand. My illness was beyond his control and temporarily beyond my control because I let it get that way.

I didn't know why I let this happen to me at the time. I chose not to call Lebanon VAMC as I was more determined than ever to get a job and keep it. Before I knew it, I was interviewing all the way from New Jersey to Center City Philadelphia. I was hired by a CPA firm outside of Philadelphia as a junior tax accountant. I was a fool to take the job, but I felt desperate inside and just because I was a MBA, they thought, and I thought, that I could handle the job without question. While I thought, working in a CPA firm would be rather interesting I was ill prepared to do it. I had never taken an income tax class in my years of study and even though I was on my way to having a MBA, that didn't prepare me to be an income tax accountant even though I really wanted it. What really blew me away was the new information system that the firm was installing. I really had no clue as to how complex doing an individual tax return on various types of software could be. Within thirty days, after a degree of manic behavior, I was asked to pack my bags and leave the firm. I won my unemployment claim against the firm. This kept me in my MBA program for a little while longer. I was totally disheartened by this time, but I was not ready to give up by any stretch of the imagination.

By now, I don't know what kept me going forward while experiencing this type of mental abuse. I couldn't accept the fact that I could not hold a job. My next stop was a bank, where I was employed as a financial systems analyst. Being that I was the hotshot MBA from the local university, the temp agency got me in at top dollar. I thought it was all going my way until I got in a conversation with another employee and I expressed that I was a bipolar. Slick move. The fellow employee came across as an incredibly intelligent lad and he also claimed that he was bipolar, but I couldn't confirm that. I just knew beyond a shadow of a doubt that I had told him that I was bipolar. Three weeks into the job I started having a slight manic swing and my work habits became slightly unorthodox. I have no conclusive evidence as to why they fired me other than the fact that I was a distraction to the rest of the workforce, and I was bringing my personal issues into the office.

Then it had to happen; the most feared aspect that I had of being bipolar: racing thoughts and information anxiety. In my case when I have racing thoughts I can absorb information so quickly that it is enough to drive me to the edge and beyond. The only thing outside of medication that has helped me in the past has been alcohol, and since I wasn't on medication the next best thing was alcohol. I would cry myself to sleep every night because this scared me into a whole new reality. Intelligence was my passion and it left me distorted. I couldn't focus or concentrate. My grades began to slip, and I began to panic with my MBA program which was my complete passion. I had to get this issue under control before too long, because I needed this degree to survive and to make it in the corporate jungle. I was not afraid to commit to self-medication at this point in my life even though it only delayed the inevitable. Oddly enough it was a beer in a public environment that made me completely realize I was driving myself in the wrong direction even though I continued along the path of self-medication for almost another year to try and control the insanity that I was experiencing. My thirst for knowledge continued. Somehow, I knew I would not be denied.

While I was self-medicating, my personal life continued on a downward spiral as I lost more and more confidence. Instead of turning to the Lebanon VAMC, I tried to create a surrogate environment in the local area using my healthcare benefits. Well, I quickly discovered that CIGNA provided the best coverage they could, but they were not a Lebanon VAMC. I did spend some time with a local psychologist who was very accommodating towards restoring my personal confidence. However, like many other independent mental health workers, she didn't understand the impact of my bipolar condition. I saw the psychologist for a number of weeks while I was going to school, and she was able to help me subdue some of my hypomanic issues and keep me focused on my studies, but she was not capable of understanding the big picture.

Finally, I searched deep within my soul and turned my faith back to the

Lebanon VAMC for guidance. You think I would have acted sooner, but I didn't. Unlike me, Lebanon acted quickly because they knew I was in dire need and referred me to Philadelphia Regional Hospital. I got a referral to see a rehabilitation team without a moment's hesitation. I was still at the point where I could maintain control sometimes, but not all of the time. I picked the worst moments to phase in and out. The rehabilitation team from Philadelphia reacted quickly. The first thing they did was send me to Bryn Mawr Rehabilitation Hospital for a neuro-psych evaluation. I must have really impressed somebody or I was taking better care of my medical condition than anybody anticipated, because scores on the evaluation were incredible. I don't recall the gentleman's name, but we seemed to get along professionally even though I thought half of his tests were a waste of time because they were so standardized throughout the industry This was 1999 and I had first seen psych testing in 1992. Basically, I had been around for a while. To make a long story short, I was probably one of the upper echelon patients that had been used to design the tests around. It is nice to brag that you are good at something other than writing books. I will have to give the evaluation team credit for one thing: they were all hotties. Jessica was my cognitive specialist and she totally blew me away without hesitation.

At this point, I thought I had escaped the world of racing thoughts. My thought process had become a true oblivion to me. Energy just continued to race through my brain at an incredible speed, and the inspirations that I came up with were either extremely efficient and idealistic, or extremely ludicrous. The one thought that incessantly burned into me was to get a job as a telecommuter. Being that I was a former officer from the adjutant general corps, I thought I could get an online job as a postmaster general for a city out west when I was on the east coast. I thought it was a brilliant idea at the time. I sent a resume for it and I waited around in my apartment long enough to get an email saying thanks, but no thanks. I couldn't do anything at a normal pace anymore...wondering if I was doing enough, not enough, or just stressing myself out. Finally, I made a command decision, gained some control, and headed back west to the Lebanon VAMC.

Part of the story I have never shared with others is what it was like for me to live in a VA lock down unit while my medical treatment team got me straight and level on medications once and for all. This is the tough part! How does this happen to an accomplished member of the academic community who has successfully completed a quality education? Most of the time, I was to be observed and my medications were to be adjusted as determined by my medical team. One night on the ward, I had begun having racing thoughts again. My RN spent time alone with me while this happened and convinced me that I needed to go out and buy a trilogy by Dr. Kay Jamison, who is a noted psychiatrist, and bipolar. I was obsessed in my quest to purchase the book at the first chance to go to Barnes and Noble. As I read her book I realized my life has mirrored hers. She went bankrupt and so did I. She wrote a series of books and I am concluding mine. Her writing is from a medical standpoint and I think mine is from a slightly more worldly viewpoint. I won't read hers again. She is a PhD and I am almost there, but not as a Psychiatrist. The question is: When will I stop being a procrastinating male and finish my book? I never believed in déjà vu'' until I started writing my book. My nurse's name was AJ and I don't know if I should say "thank you" or tell him to stay away because this has been like a bad nightmare waiting to boil over.

Well, I needed more time to adjust after a six-week stay at the Lebanon VAMC, so my social worker arranged for me to stay in a halfway house in a little town called Marietta, PA. The owner of the house was materialistic and controlling. He ran his house like a military operation, and being that I was a retired vet, this was a turnoff for me. I was never sure if he was looking out for my comfort or looking out for my pension check. Overall, I wasn't happy the way I was getting treatment, but I didn't think I was in much of a position to bargain at that point. Overall, Marietta was a beautiful little town, but the local service station wasn't exactly noted for its cheeseburgers, and all the service garages were not exactly on the up and up. It was a tough town to do business in if you had a car or if you needed new tires. There were few jobs available in Marietta either. My landlord insisted I get a job while I was under his roof and in Marietta my choice was to either be a grease monkey or to work in a foundry. Pick the lesser of the two evils.

It has always been important to me to have my own money. Living in a halfway house was the first time I didn't get to use my pension check to my benefit. It went directly to the gentleman that owned the house leaving me with nothing for myself, so I had to go out and get a job. To my chagrin, I was not allowed to drive, so I was completely dependent on the mass transit system that rolled through Marietta every day 6:45 AM. This meant taking meds before then, eating breakfast, and somehow catching the bus into the main station at Lancaster, and then catching a bus to wherever I worked. My first choice was a retail position. I thought that just because I was a MBA graduate, I should be in management right away, and not stocking shelves as a retail associate working for minimum wage. My medication made me extremely slow and hindered my communication skills. Within in a matter of a few days, I was seeking employment elsewhere as an account manager in a call center.

Once again, I was back to the routine of riding the buses and doing the changeover in the city. I must have wasted about six dollars a day just to do the transit. My job at the call center was quite unusual. I don't see why anybody wanted to purchase anything we had to sell, because it really had no value unless you had a pile of money lying around and you wanted to purchase something worthless to show for it. During the training, my medication made me fall asleep and I had to repeat the training twice. My memory was like a sieve. Cognitive rehabilitation really only pays off if you are in the right progressive environments and not being a moron. I was fortunate enough that this was about the time I got my license back and so I could concentrate on finishing my MBA at Lebanon Valley College.

I had to take two classes at Lebanon Valley College to finish my MBA and the first class was on Organizational Leadership. Discretely, I knew this was my calling and I rose to the challenge of my professor to get my Doctorate in this area. Five years later I was on track. This was 2000, and finally I was moving forward with my life even though I was still living in a halfway house (I didn't overly publicize this fact). I wanted to progress at everything I did, and I was not afraid to try. My real concern was my medication, because it made me rather clumsy and I was not exactly sure how to deal with it. But somehow I made it through the difficult times. I was getting my "drive" back and was ready to reenter the professional community after successfully completing both MBA courses needed to get my diploma from LaSalle University.

My hand-eye coordination was a major issue for me. I got the first job I wanted after leaving the halfway house, but due to my own ineptness, I was dismissed because my cognitive skills were not there. For some reason, I just could not think fast enough to prepare orders administratively to be processed through the warehouse to be picked for customers. One time I sent the wrong order and it was delivered, but the customer wouldn't take it. This was entirely my fault and I should have caught the mistake before it happened. My medication was really playing havoc with me on anything that required serious coordination and I wasn't sure what I was going to do about it. This was the job I wanted, but I wasn't measuring up to the task. Six weeks into the job, I was released. I wasn't shocked by management's decision because I was the one making mistakes. I sit here and reflect about the situation and realize that I was probably taking on too much responsibility at one time. I was always a very progressive minded person and incredibly tough on myself when failure came my way.

Two job losses in less than a year...I must have been the most determined bipolar person in Lancaster County. I was determined to get a professional job, bipolar or not. My opportunity was not to come for almost nine more months as I slaved away in the heat at Dart Container. I, like everybody else, had to pay the rent. Then the local Intermediate Unit had a job fair in which they were looking for college graduates to work as substitute teachers. At the time in 2000, I thought that this was the greatest thing that could have happened to me. Down deep within my soul, I had always wanted to be a teacher, and perhaps I was dreaming big again, but this could be the first step toward becoming a teacher once and for all. This was my dream, the fulfillment of my deepest desire, and I was willing to go the extra mile to make this happen.

So, I interviewed and yes, they hired me for a daily stipend of a hundred dollars per day, which in 2001 seemed like gold. I agreed to be a substitute teacher in IU schools and regular schools. My first day on the job was in an IU school in Lancaster City. I was bipolar and going to an inner-city school with teenagers filled with students that were suffering from mental illnesses was a major mistake for me. I was stunned. I can't imagine what I would have done if I would have been suffering from bipolar illness as a young adult. I knew how uncivil I was as an adult when my medication was not properly balanced, but I couldn't make the correlation to what these young teenagers were experiencing. I worshipped taking my medications, so I couldn't understand why anybody would potentially abuse themselves by not being on their medications. To me, being normal, like the majority of the population, was my ultimate goal.

Then I got my break. I got a call to be a district sub in a local high school. That high school called me almost on a day-to-day basis, until my medication quirked a little bit! I become rather spontaneous one day and I didn't read the teacher's directions correctly. Unfortunately, spontaneity is a bad habit for bipolars and it followed me throughout my years. I really wasn't aware of it, except that phone calls from certain school districts dwindled. Certain school districts decided not to use my services and I was not allowed to inquire as to the reason why. I learned very quickly as a substitute teacher not to share with a soul that I was bipolar. As much as we would like to think we are all open-minded and professional, there is no room for abnormalities in the schoolhouse other than in kids. I really feel for kids that are going to grow up being bipolar as adults because I found out how tough it is for a bipolar adult to survive even if you are on medication. Being aware of your own illness while you are maturing is a most incredibly difficult thing to do.

Speaking of the real world, I was living in a little town called Mt. Joy, and I was very secular in my social life. There was a little sports pub on Main Street that a CPA and I liked to frequent. Anyway, management was always friendly to me because I paid my tab, I had a good voice for karaoke, and a lot of the other patrons liked me. Then I had a slight hypomania spell one day when I was there for lunch. I kept it cool for the most part until I asked a waitress to call me an ambulance. That really bugged her out. I quickly paid my bill and left...cooling down on my own. I really should have had medical treatment, but I was very confused at the time and nobody seemed to be too concerned. Well, such is life. I went back to my house and retired for the day experiencing slight ups and downs, just hoping I would level out over in time. I was still having issues into the night when my thoughts started to race a little. I came up with an evil idea that I was determined to execute the next day. I went to my bank and took out a very large cash advance on a credit card, say about $5,000, and then I went back to the club and flaunted it in the face of the bartender. Well that got me kicked out permanently. Then like a real idiot I panicked. I had all this money and didn't know what to do with it. So, I drove a big, one-ton truck for forty miles to the VAMC to get checked into the emergency room and surrender the money to the security police in the triage. The security cop was more panicked with the money than what I was. I am really not too swift when I am on a manic swing of any type.

Needless to say, the bar was not the only place I got thrown out of before the week was out. I was going to a local church where the pastor had invited me to attend. My contributions to the plate were kind because, well, just because! For some reason, the pastor asked me to help do some volunteer work at the church: light construction, which was not exactly my forte. I was still feeling rather "manicy" at that point in time and one of the gentleman working close to me at the time heard me mumbling under my breath, and he observed me being very unmethodical about my work. In short, what I said was quickly repeated to the elders of the church and I was banned from the church. I guess mouth open, foot insert, but sometimes you can't help it. I don't fault the guy for what he did, I just don't think he made a very informed decision in dealing with my illness. Gentlemen of my nature, generally speaking, don't live in neighborhoods surrounding Mt. Joy and I was kind of getting the impression (because I had overcome a lot of my issues surrounding my illness up until 2007, when my illness began to show itself) that they didn't understand the world outside of their own little communities.

It is easy to talk about the negatives associated with being bipolar, but I had a lot of good times as well from 2000 through 2007. I showed more exuberance and energy than ninety-nine percent of the human race. The first thing I did in 2000 was get a job. As I mentioned, I went on to become a substitute teacher, which lasted until the spring of 2007. It wasn't without its pitfalls, but it served as a solid foundation of employment for almost seven years. Then, I made the decision to stay in academia. I became an adjunct professor at a local college on a one-year contract. Interesting choice of jobs, but I made the leap from secondary education to the college environment. I grew from one semester to the next. I also gained employment in Harrisburg in 2002 working for a CPA for tax season. I thought I had my temporary niche. The hours were relentless, but the overtime was great. I stayed with the firm through the spring of 2007. However, 2004 and 2005 were the years that really completed me. I enrolled in my PhD program to pursue a Doctorate of Management in Organizational Leadership and in 2005 I was hired part-time by Rowan State University to teach Business Accounting. I was on top of the world one more time. Seven years of glory and success. Then it all came crashing down when I contracted viral encephalitis from a mosquito bite.

I must be the indecision king. Sometimes the toughest decisions to me are so completely easy for someone else's gentle touch. In this case, it was my dental hygienist who led me down the path of becoming a complete intellect again, after almost a full recovery from the viral encephalitis. I wanted to blame myself for being so indecisive, but after a six-year struggle when my life was being held in the balance by a viral infection that causes traumatic brain injury, I wondered, "Why me?" It is hard to explain unless you had to live it. To voyage where very few people have ever gone and live to tell the tale of survival is something to celebrate.

My intelligence is something that I used to take for granted, even with the bipolar illness. However, 2007 really made me rethink whether I should continue to do that. My decision to write this book was made so much clearer by engaging in a conversation with someone who was wittier than me. This person took my greatest intellectual gift and caused me to somehow generate a new energy inside of me and drive me to a whole new level. She helped me recapture the events that I thought were pertinent to share with the rest of the world. I thought it was necessary to make an impact and help others understand the energy that I had to expend to move forward. Even though I am now pursuing the writing of this part of the book with great energy, it pains me to share something that nearly took my life and the struggles that I had to endure to get me back to my original baseline once again.

Viral encephalitis is an inflammation of the brain caused by a virus. Some viral diseases, such as measles and rubella, can also cause an inflammation of the brain. Other microorganisms are also capable of triggering encephalitis, such as bacteria, fungi, parasites, and mosquitoes. In my case, my medical treatment team thought it might be a mosquito, but despite the combined efforts of Lebanon and Hershey, no one will ever know for sure. Once the virus is inside the blood, it migrates to the brain and may cause traumatic brain syndrome. The brain notices the invasion of the virus and mounts a defense through the immune system, causing the brain to swell. Typical symptoms of viral encephalitis are created by the combination of infection and immune activity. As recovery occurs, the person may possibly be left with varying degrees of brain injury, which may require long-term support and therapy.

This is where I just shake my head and wonder why I put myself through the misery that I did. Was it just because I was bipolar, or did normal people have these issues too? It was October of 2007, and I was an adjunct professor of Accounting at Rowan State University in Glassboro, NJ. I was teaching Intermediate Accounting, which was quite a challenge within itself, but I loved the topic and I thought my students did as well. I was driving to the University one night on highway 322 East headed for Glassboro, when I had to stop at a three-way intersection. There was a body of swamp water off to the right, if my memory serves me correctly, which I really paid no mind to. When out of nowhere, a sports utility vehicle with an iron grill plate rammed into the rear of my Ford sedan, making it look like an accordion. I should have called 911 right away and got a police officer on the spot, but I acted spontaneously and just got out of my car and checked on the other driver first. I couldn't think fast enough to realize what kind of danger I was putting myself into. I had to be a hero and check on the other driver and do all the police officer things myself. I swapped insurance information with him and phone numbers, and drove away. It did not even dawn on me that I could not verify that the young man that had rear-ended my car had valid insurance. My little stunt of kindness and heroism was going to cost me five hundred dollars that I would never recover, a hasty decision I regretted for the next six years. If I did get bitten by an infected mosquito that night, that is where the little bastard got his opportunity and I was not even aware of it. Life has been quite challenging since 2007 and so the saga continues.

I struggled with the class that night. The easiest answers to students' questions seemed to elude me. I knew I was better than this, but I couldn't seem to function at the required level expected out of a professor of accounting. I didn't feel abnormal at this point, and even though my question and answer sessions were off focus, my dialogue was not. I always loved to talk about everything and anything. For some reason, I just was not measuring up that night to the standards of my students. Perhaps I might have been overly concerned about the damage to my car and the ensuing insurance issues that I would have to deal with for the next week or two while my car was being repaired. I took it upon myself to let the class out early that night, and I headed back to Pennsylvania only to wake up four days later in a semi-conscious state in the emergency room of the Lebanon VAMC (only my mother knows the complete truth about what happened in those four days, and I asked her not to repeat it to me because I don't think that this is a truth that my soul could bear).

ANALYSIS

The patient is a forty-year-old white male with a past medical history of bipolar mood disorder, seizure disorder, and PTSD. He was bought into the ER by his mother and stepfather after being found in his apartment in an altered mental state, unable to express himself. Mr. Mohler is a well-educated professional who is currently seeking his doctorate degree. He also teaches at a university. Prior to this recent episode, he apparently had a very high level of functioning and was able to live independently. Unfortunately, given his current mental status, agitation, and inability to speak, we cannot obtain a good history, although he is able to follow simple commands.

I heard a voice. It was the voice of an angel trying to tell me to relax. Then the torture came. Needle after needle ripped into my body and I was ready to scream out in agony. "Please help me," I thought. I couldn't even express that correctly. What did I do to deserve this agony? I heard her soothing voice again, but it meant nothing this time because my vision was clouded with anger. I had no idea what was occurring, because I had no clue as to where I was! Now hallucinations were my reality, even though they were only in my mind, telling me that my world is not being true to myself. The only thing I remembered was driving home from class, and then no recollection whatsoever. I wanted to scream at the top of my lungs, but I gagged on something in my throat. It was almost as if I was not being allowed to talk, or somebody was keeping me from biting my tongue. At this point, I was sobbing in pain. Confusion ran through my mind caused by all the pain from the needles and the IVs. Somehow, despite all this lack of clarity, I drifted off to try and catch even a minute of sleep. Then the nightmares and delusions started again and became my own worst enemy for a period of almost three weeks.

So, there I was, trapped in the pit of my own mind searching for peace and tranquility, somehow knowing that I would never have it. If I had to go through this random torture in life and survive in order to prove that I was the true Master of the Game, I didn't know if it was worth trying. If I could have given up on life at that very second, I would have without hesitation, but it was something I would never give myself the satisfaction of doing. I would not deny myself the satisfaction of living life. What else could be thrown at me other than the complete darkness I was going through? Despite the overwhelming pain and sadness that consumed me, I still believed that I was improved intellectually, morally, and became an all-around better person for being able to endure this level of torture.

Then out of nowhere it hit me: the hallucinations started when I thought my life was taking a turn for the better and my system was put into complete shock. Somehow, I awoke in a dream-like state in a state facility in Georgia. I had driven an old pick-up truck down there with the intent of selling lithium at street value. Brilliant idea for a bipolar person, right. The hallucinations did not stop there. I was arrested on a street corner by a constable with a jacket full of lithium, which the officer thought I was overdosing on. I ended up being taken to the mental ward of the local state facility for an intake session. The session was kind of brutal and the end result was that I was strapped down with leather restraints. It was weird being strapped down in my dreams and in reality at the same time. I thought I could convince the doctor to let me go once I dried out, but I could never seem to wake up from the hallucination.

Being the intellectual kid that I was, I took the position I was in literally, and thought the appropriate thing for me to do was flirt with the doctor and see if I could possibly seduce her into releasing me from this southern hellhole (I had a vivid thought process). My imagination must have been working overtime at that point; my mind must belong to the most absent-minded yet active person in the world. I wasn't going anywhere in any of the institutions I was confined in at that point in time. I never thought that puppy love could be denied in a hallucination as well. Imagine being attracted to the mind of something that existed in your mind only.

My thoughts stopped for a second. I thought I heard a voice that meant something to me. I didn't recognize it right away. My memory finally gave way. It was my mother calling out for me to wake up, but I couldn't respond. My mind was the only thing that functioned, whether it be for better or for worse. However, my body was dead to the world. Even breathing seemed irregular. She cried out for me to please wake-up, but I wouldn't respond no matter how much I was prodded. I had no energy or emotion to even react in the most basic ways. I was in a void, an endless gap that didn't allow any interaction between myself and anybody else. I still felt the restraints holding me down, and I didn't want to do anything to aggravate the IV's that were in me. There were other voices, but outside of my mother they were all blocked out. I thought I recognized one doctor's voice, but with all the pain I was in, it really didn't matter. If I would have recognized the doctor I probably would have just screamed, wanting justification as to why this was happening to me. I didn't care if they were saving my life. It just felt like pure bloody torture.

The hours turned into days and my thoughts became an endless torment. I heard laughter around, as apparently somebody was enjoying life and I wasn't. The only thing that I could recall through the mental haze that I was in was that the Philadelphia Phillies were in the World Series. The only logical thing I could follow and focus on was the cheers of the fans. I was humiliated at this point because I couldn't take care of myself. My body was just wasting away in tubes that I didn't even know the function of...other than to cause me pain. I was determined that my miserable existence would end one way or another. I had a hallucination that I was able to stand up under my own power and support myself in my weakened condition on my own two feet. What a dreamer I was. I just imagined that the floor nurse was going by my room and he/she was stunned that I was on my feet (imagine this happening when I still had my restraints on). I couldn't speak because I was so heavily medicated. Anyway, the sponge bath felt great (which was also a part of the hallucination) and then it all had to come to a grinding halt. At least I thought I was alive and kicking. At that point, reality bit me in the tail when I didn't wake up and the sponge bath didn't happen. Then the day came when I actually did wake up. I didn't have a clue as to what was going on around me, and I was shocked by my apparent situation: Helplessness. It is incredible what your imagination can do to you when you are constantly wracked with pain.

The nurses chose their words carefully as they tried to console me. I had beat death again, and there is no feeling like that when you have more faith in God than what the devil can take away from you. I had completely lost track of time, whether it be morning or evening, and I had no idea how long I had been in the hospital. I didn't even know what hospital I was in. Then she came. A female doctor, blonde hair and blue eyes, walked into my room. I didn't say a word, probably because I couldn't. Anyway, she took a seat next to me and proceeded to tell me about the past couple of weeks, and how they had almost lost me. This wasn't something that I wanted to hear, but she was telling me how it was. So, she filled me in and told me I was in the Lebanon VAMC with a viral infection. This is the part where I rolled my eyes and wondered who was teaching my classes. I guess the hospital forgot, I am a professor and I just don't check into hospitals with brain infections. This was getting better all the time. I wondered how this doctor would react if she heard my perceptions. If I could have talked, I probably would not have known what to say anyway.

After all that had happened, I just felt like telling the world that I was awake now, even though I was only somewhat aware of what was going on. However, I don't think anyone would have listened at that point. To my surprise, my whole family entered at that that moment. Everyone except for my father. His excuse was unbelievable. I couldn't even speak at the moment. The only thing I could do for the moment was suck on ice cubes as I slowly rehydrated my body. All my siblings grinned at me and said welcome back. Ironically, I didn't even know I had been gone. I couldn't remember if my mother was in tears or not, but I had never seen her so happy to see me away awake. My brother, TC, the Marine, told me to make up my mind about what I was going to do so he could go back to Iraq and win the war once and for all. Then there was my baby brother Joe. I don't exactly remember his expressions, but this is one of the few times he ever gave me a hug. Then there was my little sister, who flew in from California, where she was studying to be a nurse. I had tears in my eyes at that point, wondering what had happened to me to put so much emotional stress on my family. My cognition was not working in my favor at this point, but I was hoping it was only a matter of time until I regained full measure. I spent hours with my family that day until they reassured me that I was going to be able to move forward with the assistance of my medical treatment team. Then we all parted ways and I feebly waved to them hoping to reunite with them on a more positive note in the future.

By this point in time I was starving for some real food and the timing could not have been more perfect. As the IVs were coming out and my body was being rehydrated, I was ready to eat and get on with life. I went through a lot of ups and downs while I was hospitalized, but what really amazed me is how many friends I thought I had, but I didn't actually have. This was made evident, by the fact that only one person showed up outside of my immediate family to see me. After two hundred fifty peers that I had met in college and that I was supposedly on a first name basis with that was a batting average I didn't want on any given day. Oddly enough that one person kind of blew our friendship when he suggested that I start out my dating life with someone of my own kind. Find another bipolar doctoral candidate and then our relationship really came to a close when I decided to exercise free will and vote for whoever I wanted to in the presidential election and not who he felt was appropriate. Well he threw a fit and our friendship ended. Thus, my journey of privacy finally began. My thoughts were that I could usually ignore or overlook a lot of ignorant remarks from other people, but despite what I had been through, this person didn't measure up to me in any respect so my decision to move on with my life was the right thing to do without regard to what anyone else may think.

Finally, I was coherent enough to understand what the medical issues were that were facing me. My medical team politely informed me that I was suffering from a viral infection, which kind of kicked me where it really counted. I was used to making a living with my brain and memory, and now I was on the verge of losing full function. I was really scared of losing all the cognitive abilities that my memory had developed because I had worked so hard over the past ten years in accounting and teaching, and this required a high degree of memory work, whether you were an adjunct professor or a tax accountant. At this point in time, I didn't think this was a loss I was really equipped to handle. Ten years of hard work down the tubes and losing the overall cumulative knowledge of four college degrees. Even to this day, with all the heavy-duty hospital machines saying I have recovered from the viral infection, I feel untested even though I have developed a small business in the process. I have learned that I can still function at a much higher intellectual rate in new endeavors than I could I have imagined. I am just kind of afraid of not being able to share the intellectual powers that I once had with the foremost of my colleagues because they have discovered my weaknesses and potentially lost all respect for my leadership.

Despite all of the above, my greatest fear that really bothered me as a result of the viral infection was a loss of short-term memory. My short-term memory has left me impaired due to the inability to recall things at the intermediate level. But when it comes to my long-term memory, I hit a home run every time I go to bat provided that some part of the intermediate step is there. Not having a full awareness in that field is an issue that has plagued me for several years after I left the hospital in the fall of 2007 to resume my life out in the private community. I didn't know if I was ready to leave the VAMC, I just knew I had to take a step forward to try. I knew I was determined to try. I moved in with my mother and her boyfriend for the short-term because I was not ready to be a hero. It was a great feeling to be out of the hospital, but every time I tried to do something to improve myself, I fell flat on my face without even noticing it.

I think the toughest thing to do when you are recovering from any type of type of viral illness is to find yourself. My first real order of business was to reconnect with Rowan State University and my two classes of Intermediate Accounting. Oddly enough, if I had survived and finished the two classes, it probably would have made a major difference in my first solo business venture. The opportunity was granted to me by the department chairperson to come and visit my classes briefly. The students seemed to be somewhat stunned to see me show up in class the evenings that I did and I left with a standing ovation and the hope that I would recover soon. Then I had to meet with my boss, and after a brief discussion my employment at Rowan State was ended. Understanding how accountants operate, my boss made a conservative move, and hired a candidate that was not plagued with the medical setbacks that I had suffered.

I really was ready to give up on the teaching thing, but for some reason I could not persuade myself to do it. I just couldn't convince myself that I couldn't continue on with my career without question. I discovered that I had to be more patient with myself. I hadn't been released to drive, and fixing my car had turned into a legal nightmare due to the fact that the young man that drove the sports utility vehicle refused to pay my deductible even after my insurance company took him to court. I hadn't seen my house in three months, and only the banker knew how far behind I was on my mortgage. The University of Phoenix, where I was pursuing my doctorate, was starting to pressure me to get my dissertation completed, and only my medical treatment team knew if I was in the right frame of mind to be taking on any kind of task was mentally challenging.

Once I had assessed my current personal and professional position, I decided to extend my visit at my mother's house for six more weeks, until I truly felt strong enough to step out on my own. First stop: my house. It was springtime, and the first order of business was not to grovel in my own self-pity for a change, but to seize the bull by the horns and decide what I was going to do with my life. Teaching it was, but where? Realistically, I was damaged goods and I didn't know if I could hope for a college or university to even give me a fair nod at this point in my career. I set my sights on Stryker University as my next goal to fulfilling my teaching destiny. In the fall of 2008, I was hired as an adjunct professor of accounting and to my dismay, my medications didn't quite get the job done. By the spring of 2009, I had resigned due to a student complaint that I was starting to show a breakout of the bipolar illness once again. The student claimed I had locked myself in a classroom and was talking to myself. When I was confronted by my boss, I just hung my head in shame and resigned to avoid any future embarrassment for the school. This was the low point of my teaching career.

It was the spring of 2009, and you would think that by this point in time I would have had enough of the Good Samaritan Hospital and the Lebanon VAMC for just a little while. But this was not to be the case. It was the Spring Arts Weekend at Lebanon Valley College, and for some idiotic reason, I was asked to play in a softball game between the Knights of the Valley and KALO. I was never asked to play in any softball game during my undergraduate years, and I will admit I am the world's worst softball player, but like a hero I agreed to play. I was at the bottom of the batting order and, luckily, I got a hit. The bench for the Knights went nuts, and like the true base runner I was I nearly made it to first base. I tripped shy of first base, dislocating three fingers on my right hand. I am sure my fraternity brother was just being a good Samaritan when he took me to Good Samaritan instead of the Lebanon VAMC which left me with a surgery bill of $6,200. This shocked my system and left my checkbook stunned for the next year.

From that moment forward, I must have been in a state of grandeur. I was convinced I could live a dream, so I started a company called Trash Commanders, with the intent of recycling scrap retail tires. It was an excellent idea on paper, except I let two people influence the way I wanted to conduct my business. This was a tactical error on my part. It probably cost me the whole business by the time I fixed my mistake of listening to the wrong people. It took the wind right out of my sails. Why I didn't stick to my own instincts is beyond me. That was my biggest mistake. I made bad decisions on unfamiliar input. Being hypomanic at the time didn't help my situation either. I was making poor judgment calls using unfamiliar management tools. By the time I realized what I was doing, it was too late to correct the whole system and when I tried, it proved to be a costly mistake.

My personal spending habits went wild. I was consumed with buying things I didn't need just to say I had them. I wanted to be the Jones plus one and a half. I would go out and buy trucks just to have a different truck for every occasion such as snowplowing, construction disposal, and two one-ton trucks for tire disposal. Total personal debt on four trucks came to approximately $59,000, and then the price of fuel went through the ceiling. I was driving four beautiful trucks on fumes for almost a year financed by credit cards. Between fuel expense and misc. purchases, I spent over $80,000 in one year on credit cards. I was quite the lavish spender on fine restaurants, not being afraid to overindulge in the finest steaks on the menu. I was living the good life with no clear thought that I was headed down the path to destruction. This whole scenario was step one on the road to bankruptcy.

Secondly, I had no idea what was going wrong with me medically. I was experiencing euphoria at every corner. Nobody really knew what to do to help me, because to every extreme I exhibited tangential thinking, and I was creating a bigger financial and operational mess than I knew what to do with. There were a couple of people that really went out of their way to help me get my life reoriented. The first was my commercial landlord,

Craig. My saving grace was that when I was ill, he advertised a trailer full of used tires on Craigslist and gave away a whole tractor trailer load of tires to people who were in dire need which bailed me out financially when I needed it most. I really have to tip my hat off to Pastor Jim and his wife Wendy. When I was at my peak of experiencing tangential thinking, they kicked in and made some phone calls to the Lebanon VAMC and made the connection for me. Without Jim, I would have been sleeping in a snow bank. At this point in my life, my teaching career was over, my first stint as an independent business person had been flushed down the tubes. I learned a lot through this whole experience, and I know that I will stand firm behind whoever my medical treatment team is now and in the future of any given VAMC. However, the saga was just about to begin on so many issues that I was naïve about.

I have always considered myself to be a financial whiz kid, but I never realized how tough monetary issues were in today's financial communities until things went fiscally south for me. Things became very bad for me financially, such as pre-maturely cashing in a ton of investments and ending up owing the IRS a ton of money. For once in my life, I was really clueless until Dr. Tom Cruise (Joe Barbar) recommended that I take on a more complex issue and file for bankruptcy. The total debt that I escaped from came to approximately $450,000, due to the fact that I had gone on several manic spending sprees and outside of my business, I was out of control. The question I was faced with was whether I should fight or flee. Should I take on my debts myself, or let the legal system give me a fresh start in the world. I decided to swallow my pride and elect bankruptcy. Few other people did give me their opinions, but the decision was ultimately mine, and it was a true test of my ability to recover and think rationally again. I quickly learned that bankruptcy is a tool that worked for me, and although it is not required that anybody in my position file for bankruptcy, it is something worth investigating if you feel you are in such a difficult position.

A lot of people are stymied and struggle with the issue of budgeting which could help them deal with bankruptcies. Most people have a difficult time making a realistic budget on their own, and when I was dealing with my illness during that time period, I was no exception. On many occasions my expenses exceeded my revenues. I was not very good at exploring financial options that might have kept me out of bankruptcy. I didn't start making a budget for myself until my business was too far gone in the wrong direction, and I was in danger of losing my house because I didn't include my mortgage in my daily expenses. I just loaded one stress factor after another on myself. One of the first things I thought to do was contact a consumer credit counselor at Tabor Community

Services in Lancaster, PA to help me get my personal affairs back in order. A consumer credit counselor can help prepare a budget that will send you back in the right direction, except I was too far gone. My problem was I didn't catch the easy mistakes right away, and when I did find the right help, it was too late.

At this point in time, things were just whirling a million miles a minute for me. What was accepted financial reform and practice didn't seem to apply to me. Somehow, a large number of debt collectors managed to get hold of my personal phone number, and my time at home became a living nightmare. I was slow to get a lawyer involved at that point because I thought I could handle things with my own personal savvy (like I handled my business). A lot of debt collectors called me and tried to sell me debt consolidation loans. I approached these types of loans with a high degree of skepticism. I discovered that these types of loans are like playing double jeopardy with your personal financial situation. I learned to understand clearly that if you didn't understand the terms, interest rates, and fees associated with the loan, it was a bad investment. I realized that was just a delay in positioning myself for the inevitable. I wanted to get free of debt without incurring a balloon payment. An equity loan was not an option for me either. I had absolutely no equity in my house, and I was probably going to have a foreclosure along with the bankruptcy.

If you elect to participate in a program where a service negotiates with your creditors or makes payments on your behalf, understand whether or not the service will lower the amount you owe plus the interest rates. If this is not the case, the plan in all likelihood will fail. Some debt counselors confine themselves to dealing with your unsecured commercial creditors, excluding your obligations for non-dischargeable child support, unpaid taxes, and automobile loans. In effect, these debt counselors ignore the debts that are most important, while your money to creditors whose claims could be discharged in bankruptcy.

Bankruptcy usually results because people have problems paying their debts. They become threatened with garnishment, foreclosure, or repossession. Considering bankruptcy is not the easiest decision to make, but it may be the most plausible to help you deal with your financial problems. You have the right under federal law to file from bankruptcy relief from your creditors. Bankruptcy is a legal proceeding in which you can get a fresh financial start. Bankruptcy can be very useful and effective in resolving financial problems in many cases. However, timing is everything in filing for bankruptcy relief.

In general, you should wait as long as possible before filing for bankruptcy because you can only do it once every six years. In most cases, you should only use this valuable intellectual asset if you absolutely need it. You should openly consult with an attorney before deciding whether or not bankruptcy is right for you. There are many things that bankruptcy can do to improve your lifestyle, but you should err on the side of caution when using this privilege.

There are many things bankruptcy can do, such as eliminate the legal obligation to pay most, or all, of your debts. This is called a "discharge of debts." Bankruptcy can also stop foreclosure on your home and allow you to catch up on missed payments. It may also stop repossession of a car or other property, or in some situations, force the creditors to return the property even after it has been repossessed. However, there are a few things that a bankruptcy can't do, such as discharging debts that arise after the bankruptcy has been filed. Bankruptcies can't discharge the following debts such as child support, alimony, divorce, most student loans, and criminal fines.

Under legal advice, I ended up taking a Chapter 7 bankruptcy. A Chapter 7 is known as a "fresh start" bankruptcy, or liquidation. Your debts are discharged (cancelled) but you must give up any nonexempt property to the trustee to pay your creditors. In my case I didn't have any. You can keep secured property if you are current on the payments and continue making the payments regularly. Basically, Chapter 7 allows you to keep some of your assets if you are current on your payments. As soon as you file for a

Chapter 7 bankruptcy you will be protected from credit agency harassment. Creditors are forbidden to call you once proceedings have started. The time it takes to re-establish your credit after filing for bankruptcy is long and difficult. Don't lose faith though; the key to thinking smart from this point forward is managing your credit and give up on trying to hit homeruns (I really need to follow my advice on that one). Positive things will come in due time. This is true experience and lessons learned.

How I pulled myself out of this pit I will never know. I can attribute my success to my lawyer and my medical treatment team at the Lebanon VAMC. Thanks to them I was able to turn my life around. My lawyer got me through on the bankruptcy and my medical treatment team handled everything that said medical on it. Once again, Dr. Tom Cruise (Barbar) was the man of the hour. I mostly don't say thank you to anyone but my mother, but this time I will gladly tip my hat to the highly trained professionals of the Lebanon VAMC.

My medical troubles were only beginning to plague me. It appeared that I was still having problems with cognitive deficits through 2013. I remember many a day that I would beg for the headaches to stop and somehow for my memory to start working again. I was not at ease with myself. Every time I tried to concentrate, it was a losing battle. I was starting to lose faith in the system because, for once, my extensive research abilities couldn't find the answers and the intolerable pain that made me a jerk to be around. I was very self-centered during that period. I knew there were many veterans ahead of me that needed treatment as well, but I refused to let my voice go unheard.

I had grown to hate 2013 with a passion. Whether I could find pain due to a concussion from the car accident or the remnants of viral encephalitis. I felt that since the government had been chasing the problem since 1991 along with my own efforts there was little hope for my situation at this given point in time. Two weeks into the New Year I finally smirk for a change for the first time in almost twenty-three years.

I thought I just might have it together for the first time after I agreed to cognitive therapy at Hershey Medical Center on January 6th. This was the complete feeling that I had been waiting for. A chance to be whole again.

When I arrived at the Neuro-science clinic that day, I thought "great we are starting this with another psychiatric intake session." I wondered how long I could keep the story straight after so many different sessions from around the world. I thought we were going for a record at this point. Well, it turned out that even though the neuro-psychiatrist let me sit for a while she was pretty cool even though I was in a high degree of anticipation that day and the facts didn't deviate too much from any other psychiatric intake session because I was the one giving the story for the umpteenth time.

Just to reiterate the story, I suffered a concussion in 1991 while in the US Army that was caused within seconds of a car wreck. I suffered symptoms of HA and impairment in memory and higher executive functions such as critical thinking. Despite that, I was able to work and provide for myself until 2010 when I suffered increased stress when losing my business due to hypomanic behavior. Subsequently, I also was recovering from viral encephalitis from 2007. My bipolar behavior was controlled by 2010, but I still suffered from cognitive impairment. The main reason I had become more aggressive in seeking help through Hershey Medical Center was so that I could overcome that cognitive impairment and return to work.

Hershey and Beyond

Believe it or not, despite all the agony and torture I had been through, I was willing to go back to work. Despite all the negative innuendoes sent my way by so many people, whether it was due to the fact I was lazy or bipolar, I was still willing to go back to work. My last neuro-psych exam resulted in my having an average IQ, mild slowing of serial processing speed. Delayed memory of the 21st percentile, working memory at the 1st percentile as a result of the encephalitis and I was still willing to go back to work.

At this point in time, I had no idea how neuro-science or speech therapy were going to help me re-capture my cognitive skills, but with a degree of optimism I was willing to try. I felt that I was at the end of my rope after suffering for almost seven years from encephalitis without anybody coming up with a solution on how to treat it for me. I felt my misery had no end in sight. However, somewhere and somehow, I had faith in the system that I might find the internal fortitude that I desired. I needed to have peace within myself whether it be as an adjunct professor again or writing books. I was struggling to re-identify myself, but between the Lebanon VAMC and the Hershey Medical Center I felt that somehow I would gain peace of mind once and for all.

Every day that I approached cognitive therapy I did it with a high degree of anticipation due to the fact that I didn't know what to expect. I set my personal standards higher and higher each day, but by the same token I was afraid of failure. In one of my earliest sessions I was introduced to circumlocution which included category, function, where, and size/shape to describe an object that can't be named in conversation as a strategy for periods of anomia. At first, I was not sure what this strategy was, but after a high degree of repetition I began to see its usefulness. My long-term goals as a result of this strategy are to improve cognitive linguistic skills by 25% during functional use. This is a milestone I don't think I have yet achieved, but I am aware of the goals I have set for myself and don't expect anything lower than what I feel I can accomplish.

I thought that increasing my overall cognitive skills by twenty-five percent long term seemed to be a little bit beyond reach. But as I sit here and cross-examine myself at this point I think I can establish complete independence without too much difficulty. My clinician went on to point out that I was demonstrating good carryover of strategies taught for memory and organization from session to session. She also reports that I was using these strategies in day-to-day functioning. I demonstrated some degree of difficulty integrating attention and memory along with fine motor computer skills during a training activity on the computer. Psychomotor skills were never one of my strong suits and still aren't as a result of my deficiencies suffered from viral encephalitis. So many days went by in rehabilitation that I felt like a loser and that I was not making any true progress.

Despite my negative feelings that I had for my progress, my clinician pointed out that I was demonstrating good carryover of strategies for memory and organization on a daily basis. I began to realize the importance of using these strategies in day to day functioning and integrating all the new psycho motor skills that I had learned through the rehabilitation. I would not be denied this time, even though I was learning how to walk on a cognitive basis before I could leap.

As a result of the cognitive training, I quickly ascertained why I had opted out of law school and went on to pursue my MBA instead. My clinician asked me to complete a deductive puzzle. (Just another reason to become intellectually frustrated, it would seem). I had completed the same puzzle the day previous, but I had required assistance. Surprisingly enough I had completed the same puzzle the following day with one hundred percent accuracy in a timely manner. I was shocked in my own performance. Then came the real trick, complete a second puzzle the following day with no verbal cueing. Could I do that? Not even close. My clinician's assistance was required for me to complete the task and it left me completely befuddled.

The PQRST (preview, question, read, state, test) memory technique was reviewed to increase reading comprehension and recall of stated information. To my amazement, I was able to verbalize comprehension of this technique and begin to use it when I was reading a short news article. I started displaying signs of independence when accurately recalling specific details immediately after reading a short story with ninety percent accuracy (I had an issue with names). My clinician noted that I was able to independently state and verbalize the meanings of different words by using repetition, chunking, and association. These are short-term memory strategies used in day-to-day functioning (big words meant little to me at this point in time). I don't know if I was in complete agreement with my technician, but she thought I was demonstrating good carryover of these strategies taught for memory and organization from session to session and in my day to day functioning. I did everything I could conceptually do to master these strategies and somehow take a step back in time to help me recapture pre-morbid functioning.

PQRST technique (preview, question, read, state, test) continued to be an important factor in me developing my comprehension. It helped me in developing my reading comprehension and recall of short-term stated information. I was able to verbalize comprehension using this technique and when reading short new news articles or cross word puzzles (which I abhorred). I was given the opportunity to read a five-paragraph article for comprehension while also searching for a target word in a quiet environment. I was able to identify eight of nine target words the first time I read the article. I felt this was a major accomplishment for me thanks to the tutelage of my peer clinicians.

It is amazing how challenging and frustrating certain tasks in rehabilitation can be. I was asked to complete a planning/organizational task for attending a park with multiple time and local restrictions in place. I completed this task in ten minutes without assistance and with one hundred percent accuracy. I thought the solutions were logical and they fulfilled all given criterion. I was given an alternative attention activity which had to be completed using mathematical calculations that varied at random times. I had to be able to do this without assistance (frustration city) I maintained ninety-two percent accuracy and I required some degree of minimal assistance with this task. It was quite easy to become confused. At this point in therapy, I continued to present higher level cognitive deficits in the areas of attention, memory, and complex word finding. It was more than apparent that I would need continued therapy to provide me with new strategies to help improve my level of functioning to make me more independent. On many occasions I left the therapy shaking my head, but I was still motivated not to let the entire ordeal get the better of me.

February of 2014 was shaping up to be a tough month for my memory and abstract abilities. I had been taught a lot of new techniques that I was positive would enhance my abilities in the future, but I was so incredibly impatient in achieving these goals. I had been tasked with how to use higher level attention and deductive reasoning. After intensive tutelage, I was able to read and organize written information on a schedule with one hundred percent accuracy. I was able to read all the necessary information required to initiate a task and complete it in five minutes versus ten.

That was a major victory for me. I realized that I would have to make my life less difficult for the future. I was able to complete a basic deductive reasoning puzzle with minimal cues needed as the complexity and reasoning increased. This turned out to be a small victory for me because I was able to notice the smallest of improvements that I made for myself. My long-term goal was still to improve my linguistic skills by twenty five percent which I was beginning to think a little bit unrealistic despite the cheerleading from my clinicians. February ended with some upswings and some downswings. I continued to present higher level cognitive deficits in the areas of attention, memory, and complex word finding. It was decided that I would benefit from continued therapy including providing me with strategies that would assist me to improve to my expected level of functioning. This would allow me to excel to the most independent level of functioning possible. I had learned to be as cooperative and motivated as possible in participating at all levels of therapy, but I felt that I was somehow not reaching my fullest potential.

As therapy wore on over time, my goals changed slightly from not just improving my cognitive functioning, but to returning to pre-morbid functioning. Even today, I wonder if this is a possible reality given the trauma that I have been through. My main goal was to improve my short-term and intermediate recall. With this is mind, I was looking forward to therapy with each passing session, but I was kind of down on myself. I wanted more for myself and it wasn't coming fast enough to suit me. The progress made from simple little exercises that reviewed internal and external memory strategies didn't satisfy me, even though I excelled in them. For the first time, I learned visualization as an internal memory strategy. I was able to use verbal comprehension of all three memory strategies. However, I was not sure that I was using them in my day-to- day functioning correctly. I was at the point where I was hitting a plateau for myself and increasing my ability to function in day-to-day activities. I had gone from the point of expressing my concerns over improving my cognitive functions in utilizing my memory, to improving my "vocabulary" and "my ease of pulling out words to help me improve my overall writing skills. My clinician provided me with three different word finding exercises to complete for homework ranging from "divergent naming of abstract categories, naming multiple synonyms, and naming synonyms/antonyms." This work finally provided an elementary level of success that gave me a complete feeling of satisfaction. It laid the foundation for continual improvement on word finding skills and vocabulary as a result of the exercise. I really think I am moving forward to a new level of success. I will not be denied!

Dealing with my memory was an issue that would not escape my grasp and my clinician made sure of that. In my next wave of instruction, I was expected to master both internal and external strategies. During a question and answer session with the clinician, I noted that I routinely placed things in the same spot at home, and I use a calendar currently as reinforcement on external memory strategies. Repetition, chunking, and association were taught to help improve internal memory strategies (my clinician was getting tough on me). I was able to verbalize comprehension of these strategies after practicing several times. Mastering these three strategies at even a basic level allowed me to be more attentive and participate easier in therapy as the days went by. With the help of these strategies, I was able to learn and use several short-term memory strategies to successfully recall unrelated information, despite a gap in time and a distractor activity.

I have taken the past few months to think about the stressors that I have placed upon myself to improve my memory, whether it be short-term or long-term. I don't recall all the tests that my clinician utilized, but it made me more aware of what I must do to overcome my deficiencies. Using the learned skills of chunking, repetition, and association, I have become more aware of other people's needs and am recalling their names. I am slowly improving in the areas that I need to improve in for both internal and external issues. I have become very good at using the simple tools in life to enhance my memory and now that I have learned some basic tools to help deal with stressors, my clinician is helping me rise to the day to day challenges of grasping with the deficiencies of yesteryear. I look forward to the continued challenges that I have to deal with along with my own personal and professional progression into making me a whole person again due to the efforts of the clinicians of the Hershey Medical Center.

As I look over the past twenty-five years I have come to realize that this is only the beginning of my movement towards a complete recovery from the bipolar illness and the viral encephalitis. The challenges have been up and down and have taken their toll of me, without question. Through it all, I have always been positive and willing to give it the old college try in improving my life so that I can deal with future challenges that may come my way. I do not shirk by any stretch of the imagination, I just want the best for myself and for the others in my life. But I unfortunately have to fight the setbacks that are sometimes caused by the emotional illnesses or viral infections that I have had to deal with. Many others have had to deal with them to. Fortunately, I am in a position to write about my experiences and offer inspiration to those that need it most.

Made in the USA
Lexington, KY
04 December 2019

58034794R00155